▶   The Cultural Imaginary of the Internet

DOI: 10.1057/9781137436696.0001

Other Palgrave Pivot titles

Vanita Sundaram: Preventing Youth Violence: Rethinking the Role of Gender and Schools

Giampaolo Viglia: Pricing, Online Marketing Behavior, and Analytics

Nicos Christodoulakis: Germany's War Debt to Greece: A Burden Unsettled

Volker H. Schmidt: Global Modernity. A Conceptual Sketch

Mayesha Alam: Women and Transitional Justice: Progress and Persistent Challenges in Retributive and Restorative Processes

Rosemary Gaby: Open-Air Shakespeare: Under Australian Skies

Todd J. Coulter: Transcultural Aesthetics in the Plays of Gao Xingjian

Joanne Garde-Hansen and Hannah Grist: Remembering Dennis Potter through Fans, Extras and Archives

Ellis Cashmore and Jamie Cleland: Football's Dark Side: Corruption, Homophobia, Violence and Racism in the Beautiful Game

Ornette D. Clennon: Alternative Education and Community Engagement: Making Education a Priority

Scott L. Crabill and Dan Butin (editors): Community Engagement 2.0? Dialogues on the Future of the Civic in the Disrupted University

Martin Tunley: Mandating the Measurement of Fraud: Legislating against Loss

Colin McInnes, Adam Kamradt-Scott, Kelley Lee, Anne Roemer-Mahler, Owain David Williams and Simon Rushton: The Transformation of Global Health Governance

Tom Watson (editor): Asian Perspectives on the Development of Public Relations: Other Voices

Geir Hønneland: Arctic Politics, the Law of the Sea and Russian Identity: The Barents Sea Delimitation Agreement in Russian Public Debate

Andrew Novak: The Death Penalty in Africa: Foundations and Future Prospects

John Potts (editor): The Future of Writing

Eric Madfis: The Risk of School Rampage: Assessing and Preventing Threats of School Violence

Kevin Jefferys: The British Olympic Association: A History

James E. Will: A Contemporary Theology for Ecumenical Peace

Carrie Dunn: Female Football Fans: Community, Identity and Sexism

G. Douglas Atkins: T.S. Eliot: The Poet as Christian

Raphael Sassower: The Price of Public Intellectuals

Joanne Westwood, Cath Larkins, Dan Moxon, Yasmin Perry and Nigel Thomas (editors): Participation, Citizenship and Intergenerational Relations in Children and Young People's Lives: Children and Adults in Conversation

Jonathan Grix (editor): Leveraging Legacies from Sports Mega-Events: Concepts and Cases

Edward Webb: Media in Egypt and Tunisia: From Control to Transition?

Dayan Jayatilleka: The Fall of Global Socialism: A Counter-Narrative from the South

Linda Lawrence-Wilkes and Lyn Ashmore: The Reflective Practitioner in Professional Education

DOI: 10.1057/9781137436696.0001

palgrave▸pivot

The Cultural Imaginary of the Internet: Virtual Utopias and Dystopias

Majid Yar

Professor of Sociology, University of Hull, UK

palgrave
macmillan

DOI: 10.1057/9781137436696.0001

First published 2014 by
PALGRAVE MACMILLAN

Palgrave Macmillan in the UK is an imprint of Macmillan Publishers Limited, registered in England, company number 785998, of Houndmills, Basingstoke, Hampshire RG21 6XS.

Palgrave Macmillan in the US is a division of St Martin's Press LLC, 175 Fifth Avenue, New York, NY 10010.

Palgrave Macmillan is the global academic imprint of the above companies and has companies and representatives throughout the world.

Palgrave® and Macmillan® are registered trademarks in the United States, the United Kingdom, Europe and other countries.

ISBN: 978–1–137–43670–2 EPUB
ISBN: 978–1–137–43669–6 PDF
ISBN: 978–1–137–43668–9 Hardback

A catalogue record for this book is available from the British Library.

A catalog record for this book is available from the Library of Congress.

www.palgrave.com/pivot

DOI: 10.1057/9781137436696

▶ *For Rodanthi – who is prone to curse the internet …*

DOI: 10.1057/9781137436696.0001

Contents

DOI: 10.1057/9781137436696.0001

Note on the Author

Majid Yar is Professor of Sociology at the University of Hull UK. He has researched and written widely across the areas of crime and media, internet crime, and criminological and social theory. His recent publications include *Cybercrime and Society*, 2nd edition (2013) and *Crime, Deviance and Doping: Fallen Sports Stars, Autobiography and the Management of Stigma* (2014).

▶

palgrave▸**pivot**

www.palgrave.com/pivot

1
Unravelling Utopias and Dystopias

Abstract: *This chapter provides the broader context for this study by outlining and analysing how utopian thought has been discussed by scholars from a range of relevant disciplines (sociology, politics, philosophy and literature). Particular attention is paid to modern utopias and dystopias, and the way in which they centre upon the challenges presented by rapid social change and the place of technology in shaping human relations.*

Yar, Majid. *The Cultural Imaginary of the Internet: Virtual Utopias and Dystopias.* Basingstoke: Palgrave Macmillan, 2014. DOI: 10.1057/9781137436696.0003.

1

Introduction

It is now something of a truism that the internet has transformed social, political, cultural and economic life – from the rise of e-commerce (Castells, 2003, 2009), through the growth of new social media and social networking (Fuchs, 2013), to the use of new communication technologies in political protest and revolutionary movements (Castells, 2012; Gerbaudo, 2012). Scholarly and popular discourse addresses these developments, and presents them in contradictory ways – it imagines the internet as progress and liberation on the one hand, and as the site of risk, crime and harm on the other. This book starts with such contestation, and argues that the internet has rapidly become the space into which utopian and dystopian visions of the present and future are now projected. This imaginary, I suggest, can be located within a much broader social and cultural history, one that expresses profound ambivalence about technological change and its impact upon modern society. Consequently, in order to understand how and why we collectively imagine the internet in the ways we do, we must look beyond the past few decades and explore the cultural meanings that are sedimented around technology, and, in particular, the role ascribed to 'techno-science' in driving social change and reshaping human experience (and, indeed, potentially remaking humanity itself – Sloterdijk, 2009). This book aims to explore the meanings and narratives that shape our views of the virtual world. Its focus extends well beyond scholarly discussions to examine the wider imaginary manifest in popular culture, including film, television, novels and press reportage. In doing so, it seeks to uncover how our collective hopes, fears and fantasies about the future are now increasingly centred upon the virtual world. The concept of the imaginary used here does not imply something that is simply unreal or factually untrue – in the sense we might allude to a small child having 'an imaginary friend' or dismiss someone's anxieties by assuring them that 'you're just imagining it'. Rather, drawing upon the work of Cornelius Castoriadis and Charles Taylor, the 'social imaginary' is intended to indicate a society's 'singular way of living, seeing and making its own existence' and 'which define what, for a given society, is "real"' (Castoriadis, quoted in Thompson, 1984: 6, 22; see also Taylor, 2002). Building upon this conceptualisation, the term 'cultural imaginary' refers to the ways in which the social imaginary is given a concrete form in the sphere of cultural production

DOI: 10.1057/9781137436696.0003

and communication, manifest, for example, in the discourses of the arts, literature, film, journalism and so on.

Understanding the utopian

The social, political, philosophical, literary and artistic imaginaries of Western culture have long had, as a recurrent preoccupation, a concern with the utopian (this is not to suggest that utopian explorations are the exclusive provenance of the West, as analogous reflections are present in Chinese, Indian, Japanese, African and Islamic traditions (Sargent, 2010: 68–80); however, for present purposes, I restrict myself to discourses located within the European traditions and their various colonial off-shoots). At different times, in different discursive modes, culture has by turns projected, speculated, promised, deconstructed and satirised a world, and a mode of human existence within that world, at odds with the lived reality of the moment. 'Utopian thinking' thus maintains a compelling hold upon the ways in which we individually and collectively conceive life and its possibilities, and the ways we imagine past, present and future. Utopian thinking is always a projective endeavour in which the immediacy of the present ('what is') blurs and marries with 'what once was' and 'what might yet be'; what Northrop Frye (1965: 323) calls a 'speculative myth … designed to contain or provide a vision for one's social ideas'. To borrow from the sociologist Karl Mannheim (1997), while ideology presents the present state of human affairs as somehow inevitable, utopia gestures to other possibilities and other times. More than an amalgam or array of specific schema and blueprints (Kateb, 1963), the utopian is above all a *sensibility*, a way in which human culture understands itself and interprets and evaluates lived experience in all its ambiguities and tensions. The utopian landscapes that emerge from such exertions can be both 'positive' and 'negative' in character. They may present a clarion call for the active transformation of society so as to realise a better, more 'true' or 'authentic' mode of existence; yet they may also function as a warning (or even a counsel of despair), seeing in the process of social change the inevitability of 'decline', 'loss' and disenchantment. Whichever paths they tread, such exercises, nevertheless, shape our cultural imaginary in decisive ways, seeping into the interstices and cracks of collective

DOI: 10.1057/9781137436696.0003

consciousness, moulding our shared self-understandings in ways both subtle and profound.

This book offers some thoughts on the character of such utopian thinking at the 'twilight' of Western modernity, a period during which the accumulated impacts of rapid change and recurrent crises have shifted the contours of human experience in significant ways. It suggests that the topography of utopia is now projected into the space of the virtual, an 'other worldly' realm in which the most extravagant of possibilities are imagined. Utopia is less and less imagined as a transformation of the plane of the actual, its immanent reconfiguration into new possibilities. Indeed, the present era is one in which utopian promises of reconciliation, revolution and progress ring ever-more hollow to our ears. If, as Jonathan Glover (2001) argues, the past century was primarily one of moral atrocities (Hiroshima, the Holocaust, Soviet Gulags, Pol Pot's Year Zero and ethnic genocides) then these experiences have done much to erode the plausibility (or even the desirability) of utopian social engineering. When all attempts to realise utopian dreams end in living nightmares, and totalitarianism seems to rise recurrently from the idealistic pursuit of revolution (Popper, 2011), then grand visions of building a new society lose much of their appeal. It is this exhaustion, a sense of modernity's failed promises, which impels a new imaginary to emerge: that of a space of transcendence existing apart from a material realm whose redemptive possibilities are seen as ever-more limited and unfeasible. To borrow from Jean-Francois Lyotard (1984), the incredulity towards 'grand narratives' leaves ever-more limited space in which notions of purposive and progressive large-scale social transformation can find purchase, replaced instead by much more localised and modest *petits récits* (small narratives) around which we might organise our projects and endeavours. However, I would suggest that Lyotard was only half right; the utopian sensibility is a resilient one and is not easily lost even in the face of incredulity. Rather than simply disappearing, the utopian has been reinvigorated as it finds purchase within emerging discourses about the virtual. Our culture now imagines the internet as a space in which either the unfulfilled promises of modernity might finally be realised (liberation, self-transformation, solidarity, equality) or one in which such dreams find their final dissolution as the humanist vision is lost in a realm of technological hybridisation, alienation and domination. Both sides of this fevered, extravagant sensibility recode and replay the dialectical turnings of modernity: Rationalism and Romanticism,

DOI: 10.1057/9781137436696.0003

Technology and Nature, progress-as-loss and progress-as-redemption. It is only by critically reflecting on our cultural discourses about the virtual world in this way that we can begin to grasp why and how the virtual has become the utopian space of our times.

Recent scholarship in the human sciences has taken utopianism, those modes of thinking associated with the speculative projection of possible human worlds, as a distinctive object of analysis and interrogation. My aim here is not to systematically survey this scholarship – there are many informative works that do just this (see, for example, Kumar, 1997, 1991; Sargent, 2010; Levitas, 2011). Instead, I have drawn selectively upon this literature so as to delineate some important features of what I take to characterise utopian thinking. As early as 1936, Karl Mannheim discussed what he termed the 'utopian mentality', by which he meant a 'state of mind' that 'is incongruous with the state of reality in which it occurs'(Mannheim, 1997: XX). Thus a first important feature of the utopian sensibility is its extrapolative quality, its conceptualisation of a world that is not simply derivable from the empirically available context in which that thinking occurs: it imagines a world different from, and often at odds with, the 'actually existing' social and historical conditions in which it takes place. A second noteworthy feature of utopianism is recapitulated by Bauman (1976) who notes that utopia functions in an ambiguous space of double meaning: it can refer both to u-topia, 'a place which does not exist', and to eu-topia, a good place, 'a place to be desired'. This dual meaning can be traced to the first use of the term itself, in Thomas More's *Concerning the Best State of a Commonwealth and the New Island of Utopia: A Truly Golden Handbook No Less Beneficial Than Entertaining* (1516), now better known as *Utopia*. These two senses of utopia have in time come to be conjoined, and it 'has come to refer to a non-existent good place' (Sargent, 2010: 2). Thus at the heart of utopianism's projective movement is a *normative* core: it is bound-up with the perennial attempt to imagine 'the good life'.

A third element crucial for our understanding of the utopian is identified by Foucault (1967) in his well-known essay on heterotopias. He views such heterotopias as

> sites that have a general relation of direct or inverted analogy with the real space of Society. They present society itself in a perfected form, or else society turned upside down, but in any case these utopias are fundamentally unreal spaces.

DOI: 10.1057/9781137436696.0003

In other words, utopias, for all their disjunction from 'the real space of Society', nonetheless, always have their roots in that very space: their disjunctive quality arises from the ways in which they break with a lived reality that fundamentally defines them. Precisely for this reason all variants of utopia reflect and respond to the issues and concerns that predominate in society at the time of their composition. For example, the contours of the future society envisioned by William Morris in *News from Nowhere* (1890) – such as common ownership, democratic self-determination, the abolition of private property and the collapse of class distinctions – is an 'inverted analogy' of the capitalist England of the author's time.

Claeys and Sargent (1999) give us useful insights into utopias as modes of 'cultural production'. They define all utopian cultural discourses as 'the imaginative projection, *positive or negative*, of a society that is substantially different from the one in which the author lives' (emphasis added). Important here is the claim that utopias are *not* co-extensive with eu-topias – utopian constructions cannot be confined to those that depict a desirable state of affairs. In fact, both 'good' and 'bad' (dystopian) imagined worlds are variants of utopian thinking. Indeed, they point out that it is by no means a straightforward business to determine whether a particular imagined unreality is meant as a positive (eu-topian) or negative (dystopian) representation. A prime example of this indeterminacy is one of the most famous products of the utopian canon, Thomas More's *Utopia* (1516). On the one hand, More's *Utopia* can be read as a positive projection of a better society, the depiction of an ordered society that furnishes a pointed contrast to 'the chaos of sixteenth-century life in England' (Frye, 1965: 325). On the other hand, it can be understood as a satire of radical and 'heretical' views that circulated in Europe at the time of writing. For example, More's imagined society features married priests, female priests and the abolition of private property – these would seem to be antithetical to an author who was a devout Catholic, enthusiastic persecutor of Protestant 'heretics' , and one of England's major land owners. The suspicion that Utopia's social order is the subject of mockery rather than commendation is furthered when we realise that More indulges in sly word plays – for example, the name given to the visitor who describes the island is Hythlodaeus, which in Greek means 'distributor or speaker of nonsense' (Wilson, 1992: 33; Sargent, 2010: 22).

DOI: 10.1057/9781137436696.0003

Claeys and Sargent further distinguish between two 'modes' of utopian thinking. The first looks backwards towards an imaginary past in which life was 'different' and 'better'. This utopia is often a kind of prelapsarian paradise, imagined as Eden, Arcadia and suchlike. In its setting, a 'natural' or 'spontaneous' life is enjoyed, one of sensual gratification, solidarity, harmony, community, plenitude or innocence. One of the earliest such utopias is that of the Golden Age (Χρυσόν Γένος) which is commonly attributed to the Greek poet Hesiod (and later reworked by the Roman poets Virgil and Ovid). In his *Works and Days* (dated to the 6th century BC), Hesiod depicts the 'Five Ages of Man', starting with the Golden Age. In this first Age,

> ...they lived like gods and no sorrow of heart they felt.
> Nothing for toil or pitiful age they cared,
> But in strength of hand and foot still unimpaired
> They feasted gaily, undarkened by sufferings.
>
> (Hesiod, quoted in Claeys and Sargent, 1999: 7)

Such utopian representations are characterised by two particularly notable features. First, the life of ease and abundance is portrayed as a gift to Man from Nature, the gods or God – in this case, it is presided over by the Titan Kronos, son of Uranus and Gaia, and father of Zeus (and ends when the Titan is overthrown by his son). Second, this earliest incarnation of human existence is depicted as the best possible such life, and in the mythic history offered (such as Hesiod's Five Ages) subsequent eras are imagined as a decline from utopian beginnings – from an original state of peace and plenitude, Man is cast into a life of hardship, want, conflict, war and suffering:

> Fifth is the race that I call my own and abhor
> O to die, or be later born, or born before!
> This is the Race of Iron. Dark is their plight.
> Toil and sorrow is theirs, and by night.
>
> (Ibid.)

This narrative sequence, leading from perfection to corruption, may be reasonably presented as the prototype of Christianity's tale of the Fall and Man's expulsion from Eden (Delumeau, 2000: 6–7). This 'paradise lost' may be ritually recaptured in schema that promise at least a temporary restoration of the imagined ideal past. Examples include the Roman festival of Saturnalia (honouring the god Saturn), which offered to recapture

DOI: 10.1057/9781137436696.0003

the conditions of the Golden Age, including its egalitarianism (Roman masters would wait upon their slaves) and bountiful indulgence in the pleasures of feasting, intoxication and gambling (Frazer, 2009: 631–2). The spirit of the Saturnalia was later recuperated into the Medieval Christian 'Feast of Fools' (Harris, 2011) and the tradition of Carnival (Gardiner, 1992). Indeed, it has been argued that the reactivation of an original state of fulfilment is still evident in a range of contemporary social and cultural practices, spanning the Mardi Gras of New Orleans (Gotham, 2005), seaside holidays (Webb, 2005) and the social protests of the Occupy movement (Tancons, 2011).

The second 'mode' of thinking is very different: it looks not to utopia as the restoration of a natural condition now lost in the past, but imagines utopia as the intentional product of rational action, the outcome of 'human contrivance' or social 'engineering' through which the good society might be realised in the future. Here, utopia is fabricated through an alliance of rational planning and human will, the outcome of concerted agency (an achievement of what Hannah Arendt (1999) calls *homo faber*, the human capacity to create and build a world that is not 'given'). Such utopian fictions are instances of what Raymond Williams (1978: 203) calls '*the willed transformation*, in which a new kind of life has been achieved by human effort'. An illustrative early example of such a utopian construct is, of course, Plato's *Republic*. Plato's ideal state, *Kallipolis* (literally the 'good city') is ruled by a caste of philosopher-kings whose pursuit of the good is grounded in their dedication to wisdom, which in itself is conceived as an awareness of the ideal forms: they possess 'knowledge of the true being of each thing' and so have 'perfect vision of the other world to order the laws about beauty, goodness, justice' (Book VI). In a significant sense Plato provides a template for all later utopias that are called into being through rational action. Such engineered utopias come into their own under the aegis of Enlightenment modernity; it is the distinctive belief in human agency and reason, the ability of human beings to purposefully effect social progress through wholesale transformation, which inspires many such utopian visions. However, modern utopias of this kind differ markedly from that of Plato insofar as they depend on a very different concept of reason. Far from the contemplative apprehension of eternal and metaphysical truths so beloved of Plato, modernity's reason is grounded in what Francis Bacon called the *Novum Organum*, the 'new method' of scientific reasoning that is tied to the pursuit of empirical knowledge through observation and experimental inquiry. Reason of

DOI: 10.1057/9781137436696.0003

this kind could reveal the underlying workings of nature, which in turn could be directed in the name of human betterment and progress (Bacon, 2009). Three years after the publication of his *Novum Organum* in 1620, Bacon produced a utopian novel that sets out the society that could be built upon the foundations of scientific reason – *New Atlantis*. On the island of Bensalem, it is the scientists who furnish the basis for order, prosperity and peace through their accumulation of knowledge – 'The end of our Foundation is the Knowledge of Causes, and Secret Motions of Things; And the Enlarging of the bounds of Humane Empire, to the Effecting of all Things possible' (Bacon, 2006: 75). As Sibley (1973: 262) notes:

> the *New Atlantis* is devoted to a somewhat detailed description of technological discoveries – a veritable encomium on man's power to understand Nature and then to dominate it. There are caves for refrigeration. Submarines go to the depths of the ocean. Men imitate birds and fly through the air. Mile-high towers observe the weather. A device has been invented to magnify the human voice.

As we shall see in subsequent discussions, this marriage of scientific reason and human endeavour, realised through technological innovation, is a central feature of modern utopias, and plays a particularly important role in the constructions of virtual utopias in the era of the internet.

Returning to the variants of utopian thought, it is further apparent that different utopian schemes have tended to flourish at different points in the cultural history of Europe. Claeys and Sargent (1999) identify four such distinctive forms of utopian constructs that have figured in the cultural imagination of the West since the early modern period.

First, the 16th and 17th centuries saw an upsurge of religious utopianism which linked Christianity with communistic egalitarianism, and produced a number of notable works. Examples include *The City of the Sun* (1602), written by the 'heretic' Dominican theologian Tommaso Campanella, which imagined a theocratic city in which women, children, food, homes and all other forms of property were held in common (Campanella, 2008). In a secularised form these in turn inspired the small-scale communal socialism associated with the likes of Charles Fourier and Robert Owen. Twentieth-century experiments in communal living (what Roberts (1971) dubbed the 'new communes') can also be seen as reiterations of this utopian socialism, seeking to create a collective existence oriented to 'ends involving harmony, brotherhood, mutual

DOI: 10.1057/9781137436696.0003

support, and value expression' (Kanter, 1972: 2). Such communal utopias typically emphasise small-scale social organisation, placing particular importance upon the bonds of intimacy enabled by face-to-face interaction and close-knit relations.

A second form of utopian vision was connected to the so-called voyages of discovery associated with European imperial expansions. Travellers' tales and proto-anthropological accounts of newly discovered 'primitive' cultures (Cook, 1999) activated the ideal of living in uncorrupted simplicity; here we find the stimulus for the Romantic figure of 'le bon sauvage', the 'noble savage' (Ellingson, 2001). Undoubtedly, the valorisation of the 'primitive' other served as a critical mirror in which the perceived ailments of European societies could be sharply delineated: 'natural goodness versus the corruption of European society, oneness with nature versus European estrangement from it, individualism versus social bonds, untutored wisdom versus sophistication, and equality versus European social hierarchy' (Liebersohn, 1994: 746). Such utopianism, with its focus upon the virtues of a 'natural' existence, was certainly fuelled by Romanticism which placed emphasis upon imagination, emotions, myth and intuition. This Romantic sensibility would later re-emerge in dystopian critiques of modern industrial society.

Third, we see the emergence in the 19th century of 'utopias of justice and equality', which transfigure the small-scale socialism of earlier utopianism into a vision of large-scale social transformation. In such utopias, industrial production and modern instrumental rationality are appropriated for the benefit of all, so as to enable the building of a society characterised by both equality and plenitude. Amongst the most important utopian works in this tradition we find Edward Bellamy's *Looking Backward: 2000–1887 A.D.* first published in 1888. In his future vision of Boston, corporate industrialism has been nationalised, co-operation has replaced competition and the maximising of efficiency enables all to enjoy an equal share of the goods produced (Tilman, 1985). In Bellamy's (1996: 142) words:

> With a tear for the dark past, turn we then to the dazzling future, and, veiling our eyes, press forward. The long and weary winter of the race is ended. Its summer has begun. Humanity has burst the chrysalis. The heavens are before it.

The place of industrialism in the configuration of modern utopias brings us to a fourth mode of thinking, that which is associated with

DOI: 10.1057/9781137436696.0003

techno-scientific utopias. These quintessentially modern utopias promise indefinite progress and material abundance enabled by the development of science and technology, and the ultimate 'defeat' of pain, disease and even death itself. The scientific rationality espoused by Bacon is allied to the dynamic possibilities unleashed by the Industrial Revolution, creating a vision of a society transformed by the power of the machine. The machine, as technology materialised, is both literally and metaphorically the *engine* that propels change, relieving people of the burden of productive labour, thereby making possible a life of pleasure, sociability, contemplation and so on (Sippel, 2006). As the 19th-century French revolutionary Etienne Cabet put it in his utopian novel *Voyage en Icarie* (1842):

> The present limitless development of the power of production thanks to the use of steam and machinery... can bring *equality of abundance*, and no other system is more favourable to the perfecting of arts and the reasonable pleasures of civilization. (quoted in Sibley, 1973: 266)

Speculative projections of this kind proliferated from the 19th century onwards, as a belief in technology as the key to social and economic advancement became central in industrialising societies' visions of progress. Raymond Williams (1978: 203) notes that the literary genre of science fiction is founded in significant part upon the narrative device of a '*technological transformation* in which a new kind of life has been made possible by a technical discovery'. This imaginative appropriation of techno-science also finds its inverted form in the proliferation of modern dystopias. Like the utopianism noted above, technology occupies a central place in revolutionising society, but does so from the perspective that 'the conditions of life have been worsened by technical development' (Ibid.: 204). Beginning with the Romantic reaction against Enlightenment rationalism, typified by Mary Shelley's *Frankenstein* (1817), techno-scientific dystopias remain a recurrent and increasingly dominant feature of modern cultural production. In both their 'positive' and 'negative' incarnations, techno-scientific utopias create the fundamental template for contemporary utopias of the virtual realm.

DOI: 10.1057/9781137436696.0003

2
The Techno-Scientific Utopias of Modernity: From Real to Virtual

Abstract: *Building upon the introduction in Chapter 1, this chapter focuses on the cultural rendering of modernity's 'techno-scientific' utopias. Through an exploration of works of both 'social science' and 'science fiction', Chapter 2 explores how modern culture has built projective fantasies about the future around technology's power to transform human existence. It is suggested here that more recent contributions to this cultural tradition (e.g., the speculative works of Iain M. Banks, Neal Asher, Isaac Asimov and William Gibson) mark a shift in which technological utopias are now projected into the world of the virtual.*

Yar, Majid. *The Cultural Imaginary of the Internet: Virtual Utopias and Dystopias*. Basingstoke: Palgrave Macmillan, 2014. DOI: 10.1057/9781137436696.0004.

The concluding discussion in Chapter 1 sets the scene for a more detailed consideration of the development of techno-scientific utopianism, and the way it configures imaginaries of the virtual. However, before we can engage in this exploration, we need to note the complex ways in which utopian constructions combine and inter-mingle elements from different modes of thought. I have already set out Claeys and Sargent's four-fold classification of modern modes of utopian thinking – those derived in turn from religious radicalism, romantic 'primitivism', socialist egalitarianism, and the Enlightenment faith in the techno-scientific. However, these ought to be seen as at best a form of ideal–typical analysis. In actuality, we find that particular utopian discourses marry elements drawn from different streams of utopian thinking. Consider, for example, the writings of H.G. Wells, which we shall discuss in some detail. At one level his *oeuvre* can be read as a positive utopianism situated firmly in with the techno-scientific imaginary of European modernity. Science and technology, and the application of scientific rationality, are for Wells a means to make a good society. Thus it is no coincidence that Wells was an enthusiastic proponent of eugenics. The term was first coined by the biologist and psychometrician Francis Galton, who saw in Darwin's account of evolution the possibility of improving humanity through selective reproduction. Such practices, he proclaimed, were the means by which 'the Utopias in the dreamland of philanthropists may become practical possibilities' (Galton in Parrinder, 1997: 2). Indeed, he wrote an incomplete utopian novel, *Kantsaywhere*, which imagined a society built upon eugenics. Like many of his fellow Fabians, Wells embraced the idea that the rational manipulation of human genetics could help create a society that is healthier and happier than ever before (Paul, 1984). Yet Wells also draws clearly and consistently upon the traditions of egalitarian socialism, emphasising in his utopian writings pacifism, world government and distributive equality. However, there is also an element of the ethical naturalism of older utopian roots, with his endorsement of 'free love' (Lodge, 2012). Nevertheless, as we shall see below, for a wide and diverse range of utopian thinkers of 19th and early 20th centuries, techno-science offers the key to social progress and the betterment of humanity.

The technological utopias of social science

It would not be implausible to suggest that the birth of the social sciences, especially the discipline of sociology, is closely bound up with

DOI: 10.1057/9781137436696.0004

utopianism (Jacobsen and Tester, 2012: 2), especially that of the techno-scientific variety. Both in very project of developing a 'science of the social', and in that science's emergent visions of social change and human progress, technological utopianism plays a pivotal role, and so takes its place alongside more literary speculations of the same temper. Here I will consider the place of technological utopianism within the work of three pivotal thinkers, Henri de Saint-Simon, Karl Marx and Friedrich Engels.

Saint-Simon is little regarded, and even less frequently discussed, in contemporary sociology, other than as a precursor of more important figures, such as Auguste Comte, who were influenced by his writings (indeed, Comte acted as secretary and collaborator to Saint-Simon for a number years – Simon, 1956: 312). He is most often identified as a 'proto-positivist' who outlined the project of a 'science of society' that could utilise careful empirical observation so as to reveal the general laws that drive and shape human history (Lyon, 1961). This is the limit of the noteworthiness he is accorded in textbooks of sociology, which typically attribute to him the first moves in the development of 'positive philosophy', but otherwise dismiss him as 'eccentric', 'confused' and 'unsystematic' (see, for example, Fulcher and Scott, 2007: 24). Yet his faith in science and scientific method extends well beyond the goal of establishing the intellectual tools needed to place historical knowledge on an objective and universal footing. Saint-Simon equally occupies a significant place in the development of modern utopian discourse. He figures as a prominent voice in 19th-century socialist utopianism, offering a vision of progress that is rooted in technological innovation. In Saint-Simon's anticipation of the future, scientists replace priests as the ultimate arbiters of truth, as they would guide 'man's mission to transcend nature with technology' (Ophuls, quoted in Krier and Gillette, 1985: 407). For the government of the new society, he proposes the establishment of a tricameral 'industrial parliament' in which engineers, mathematicians and physicists will have the predominant representation in its two highest chambers; the third will comprise 'captains of industry' whose role it is to enact the directives and decisions issued by scientists, which will be aimed solely towards the betterment of human existence through the application of scientific knowledge (Booth, 1871: 52). For Saint-Simon, revolutionising society along these lines would 'culminate ... in the full realization of mental and moral powers in a totally reconstituted and emancipated world' (Kumar, 1991: 30). This vision of a

DOI: 10.1057/9781137436696.0004

techno-scientific society, mediated particularly through Comte's account of industrial progress, exercised a decisive influence over thinkers such as Marx and Durkheim (Stedman-Jones, 2006).

The label of 'utopian' was something Marx (alongside Engels) robustly resisted; in their view, 'utopias were speculative and fanciful; their thinking on the contrary was scientific ...' (Ibid.: 60). The science of historical materialism offered an objective account of the dialectical development of human society, and neither needed nor required the kind of wishful thinking associated with utopian dreamers. Marx and Engels were thus at pains to distinguish their 'scientific socialism' from its utopian forbears. Yet Marx and Engels propose a sweeping account of historical transformation that culminates in the end of history, the abolition of class distinctions, the transcending of inequality and conflict and the overcoming of alienation. The process leading to the creation of communist society may be based in the iron-clad interplay of material forces, but the end point is envisaged in clearly utopian terms. For example, in one of the most famous passages from *The German Ideology*, Marx and Engels (2004: 54) proclaim that:

> In communist society... each can become accomplished in any branch [of activity] he wishes, society... makes it possible for me to do one thing one day and another tomorrow, to hunt in the morning, fish in the afternoon, rear cattle in the evening, criticise after dinner, just as I have a mind.

There can be little doubt, his protestations notwithstanding, that Marx's communist society is amongst 'the most famous of utopias' (Ollman, 2004). However, this is no bucolic idyll akin to the return-to-nature fantasies of Romantic poets. On the contrary, reconciliation, peace, plenitude and solidarity are built upon the powers of industrial technology first harnessed (to terrible human cost) by capitalism. In this future:

> Technology has developed to a plane where practically anything is possible. Wastelands have been brought under cultivation; a multitude of modern towns have sprung up in the countryside; large cities have been renovated; the communication and transportation systems are as advanced as anything we now have. (Ibid.)

The Marxist utopia is a quintessentially techno-scientific achievement, one which 'sees techno-science as a central agent in a dialectical drama culminating in the inevitable defeat of capital' (Dyer-Witherford, 1999: 38).

DOI: 10.1057/9781137436696.0004

The technological utopias of science fiction

Alongside the anticipations of social progress envisioned in the social sciences, the 19th century also initiates similarly scientifically oriented utopian projections in the literary arts. In particular this period sees an upsurge in speculative fiction (later dubbed 'science fiction') that imagines possible future or alternative worlds that have been transformed by techno-science. Modernity, science and social transformation lie at the heart of the genre and drive much of its concerns:

> Science fiction...developed as part of industrial society. It is intrinsically linked to the rise of modern science and technology, growing with these forces, reflecting and expressing them, evaluating them, and relating them meaningfully to the rest of human existence. (Franklin, 1995: 1)

Identifying a clear point of origin for science fiction has proven to be a rather contested endeavour; some critics and literary historians identify Mary Shelley's *Frankenstein* (1818) as the first work of proper science fiction (Aldiss, 1973; Malmgrem, 1991), while others see clear proto-science fictional themes in much earlier poetic and mythical works (Roberts, 2000). However, setting aside the traditions of 'scientific romance' and adventure (associated with the likes of Jules Verne), we can suggest that H.G. Wells is 'the pivotal figure in the evolution of...modern science fiction' (Parrinder, 1980: 10), and it is in his works that we see the utopian and the scientific articulated together in a concerted form.

Over the course of his literary career, spanning almost 50 years, Wells explored the utopian (and sometimes dystopian) implications of modern techno-science. In *Anticipations of the Reaction of Mechanical and Scientific Progress upon Human Life and Thought* (1901), he anticipates radical social transformations that will be wrought by new communication and transport technologies, reshaping the structures and patterns of human existence. In *A Modern Utopia* (1905), two English travellers in the Swiss Alps are transported to the distant planet of Utopia, where they embark upon a journey to discover the workings of its society. In addition to Wells' familiar socialist themes (world government, common ownership via the state, gender equality and the transcendence of material want), the novel dwells on the role of scientific and technological progress in the making of Utopia:

> development of new machinery, the discovery of new materials, and the appearance of new social possibilities through the organised pursuit of

DOI: 10.1057/9781137436696.0004

material science, has given enormous and unprecedented facilities to the spirit of innovation. (Wells, 1905: 19)

> Utopian economics is ... the most efficient application of the steadily increasing quantities of material energy the progress of science makes available for human service, to the general needs of mankind. (38)

> ... the new conditions physical science is bringing about, not only dispense with man as a source of energy but supply the hope that all routine work may be made automatic, it is becoming conceivable that presently there may be no need for anyone to toil habitually at all. (43)

Well's 1923 novel *Men Like Gods* employs a similar narrative device wherein the narrator, Barnstaple, is transported to a distant world also called Utopia, which is depicted as a projection of Earth thousands of years into the future. While the world state of *A Modern Utopia* is replaced here by a kind anarcho-socialism, the themes of human progress through techno-science remain a consistent feature:

> A vigorous development of scientific inquiry began and, trailing after it a multitude of ingenious inventions, produced a great enlargement of practical human power ... physiological and then psychological science followed in the wake of physics and chemistry, and extraordinary possibilities of control over his own body and his own social life dawned upon the Utopian. (Wells, 1923: 67)

Wells in many senses established the template for early science fiction's imaginary of utopian social progress driven by scientific advancement. Other notable contributions in this vein are manifold, including those of Hugo Gernsback, founding editor of the first science fiction magazine, *Amazing Stories* in 1926, which published amongst others H.G. Wells (Westfahl et al., 2007); John W. Campbell, editor of *Astounding Science Fiction* (Landon, 2002); and E.E. 'Doc' Smith, pioneering author of extravagant technology-driven 'space operas'. However, one contribution especially noteworthy for its embodiment of scientific optimism is Isaac Asimov's seven-volume *Foundation* series, published between 1942 and 1993. The novels are set in a far-future galaxy-spanning Empire, which is made possible by instantaneous faster-than-light travel. The narrative centres upon the scientist Hari Seldon, who invents a new discipline of 'psychohistory', a kind of mathematical sociology that enables him to accurately predict the future development of humanity. When his predictions indicate the onset of an imminent Dark Age, he establishes a Foundation whose members will be the custodians of knowledge and Enlightenment, and who will sow the seeds for a renewal of civilisation.

DOI: 10.1057/9781137436696.0004

Seldon reappears periodically after his death in recorded form, offering his followers guidance based upon his scientific predictions of the future. A further key theme in the latter books of the sequence is a benign and humanistic vision of artificial intelligence, with robotic humanoids playing a central role in preserving and advancing human culture (a matter to which we shall return shortly). Science fiction novelist Frank Herbert astutely noted that in Asimov's vision:

> History...is manipulated for larger ends and for the greater good as determined by scientific aristocracy. It is assumed, then, that the scientist-shamans know best what course humankind should take...it is assumed that no surprise will be too great or too unexpected to overcome the firm grasp of science upon human destiny. This is essentially the assumption that science can produce a surprise-free future for humankind. (Herbert, in Roberts, 2000: 78)

Another variant of this 'surprise free' techno-scientific utopianism can be found in the fictional writings of the behaviourist psychologist B.F. Skinner. In *Walden Two* (1948), Skinner envisages a modern utopia of health, friendship and balance brought about by the interventions of behaviourist science. The idealised community is rationally planned using scientific principles, and social problems are resolved through scientific problem-solving and use of the experimental method so as to objectively reveal the optimal solution. Child-rearing in conventional family structures is deemed both inefficient and ineffective (producing maladjusted individuals), so children are raised communally under the supervision of trained behavioural scientists who can ensure that progeny are fully integrated into the social order and content with their place in it. The eugenics of Wells and the behaviourism of Skinner, of course, find their negative inversion in Huxley's dystopia of *Brave New World* (1932) – a work which we shall consider further in Chapter 4.

The kinds of techno-scientific optimism that energised early science fiction began by the mid-20th century to be noticeably displaced by darker visions about the future development of society. It has been suggested, entirely reasonably, that visions of technological empowerment and human betterment started to lose their persuasiveness in the wake of history's counter-lessons: the birth of mechanised warfare in World War I (WWI); World War II (WWII) which saw wholesale devastation through Blitzkrieg and carpet-bombing, the monstrous perversion of technological efficiency in the Holocaust's gas chambers, and the birth

DOI: 10.1057/9781137436696.0004

of the 'atomic age' in the destruction of Hiroshima and Nagasaki. The socialist faith in industrial advancement as the path to equality and freedom from want faltered in the face of Stalin's disastrous collectivisations and purges. Correspondingly, the period after WWII sees the waning of techno-scientific utopian projections of the kind pioneered by Wells, and the rise of dystopian works of science fiction such as Nevil Shute's *On the Beach* (1957) and Walter M. Miller's *A Canticle for Leibowitz* (1960), both of which explore the post-apocalyptic devastation left by nuclear war; Kurt Vonnegut's *Player Piano* (1952) (also published under the title of *Utopia 14*), which focuses upon the dehumanising effects of technological automation; and Richard Matheson's *I Am Legend* (1954), in which war causes a pandemic that turns its victims into vampires. The techno-dystopian imaginary will be explored in detail in Chapter 4; for the moment it is sufficient to note the declining appeal of scientific utopianism in the post-WWII context. This is not to say that utopian fictions as such either ceased to appear or ceased to resonate with the sensibilities of the public. On the contrary, the political and cultural ferment of the 1960s both inspired and was in turn inspired by a number of popular utopian fictions (Baccolini and Moylan, 2003: 2). Examples include the 'counter-cultural' paganism of Robert Heinlein's *Stranger in a Strange Land* (1961) (Cusack, 2009); the ecological utopianism of Ernest Callenbach's *Ecotopia* (1975); and Ursula Le Guin's feminist utopian novel *The Left Hand of Darkness* (1969). However, the techno-scientific is either marginal to such utopias, or seen as an active impediment to their realisation. It is not until the 1980s that techno-scientific utopianism returns to the frontlines of speculative fiction, in a new and reconfigured form.

Techno-scientific utopias of the virtual

Terms such as 'the virtual', 'virtual reality' and 'virtuality' have gained common currency in recent decades, and have been used in a variety of senses and contexts. In its narrow specification, it is used to describe 'computer systems that create a real-time 3D audio and visual experience depicting a simulation of reality or an imagined reality' (Bell et al., 2004: 178). More broadly, it has become a short-hand for the totality of 'spaces' generated by computer-media interaction, including the internet and World Wide Web (see, for example, Turkle, 1996). In this discussion, I

DOI: 10.1057/9781137436696.0004

extend the terminology to also include the actual, emergent, anticipated and imagined 'smart' technologies, including Artificial Intelligences (A.I.s) and cybernetic organisms ('cyborgs') associated with the near-exponential growth of computational power and flexibility that has taken place over the recent past. In the early 1960s, the scientist and entrepreneur Gordon Moore predicted 'that circuit densities of semiconductors had and would continue to double on a regular basis' (Schaller, 1996) producing an accelerating upward curve in the information-processing capabilities of computers (this prediction has been borne out, and has commonly come to be known as 'Moore's Law'). This development furnished not only the technological basis of the so-called computer revolution, but has also driven the development of A.I. research, which seeks to engineer 'intelligent machines' that 'in some way mimic or replicate human thought and behaviour processes' including 'game-playing... mathematical problem-solving, language use, translation and reasoning... medical diagnosis and conversation' (Bell et al., 2004: 7). Moreover, 'other human traits, such as emotion and empathy, have also been replicated (or impersonated) by AIs, leading to a further blurring of the human-machine distinction' (Ibid.). Such innovations have also provided a fertile ground upon which a new wave of techno-scientific utopians could imagine a future transformed through the rise of the virtual. Here I will explore the iteration of such 'virtual utopianism' in the work of four authors, Iain M. Banks, Neal Asher, Isaac Asimov and William Gibson.

Iain M. Banks' contribution to the discourse of what I call 'virtual utopianism' takes the form of his series of best-selling 'Culture' novels. Starting with *Consider Phlebas* (1987) and continuing through nine subsequent books, Banks articulates a distinctive utopian vision. At one level, his Culture is recognisably influenced by the technological utopianism of Asimov and the socialist utopianism of Wells. The Culture, a galaxy-spanning civilisation of some 30 trillion persons, is anarcho-socialist in its politics; it has neither a state nor corporations. When collective decisions need to be made, they are agreed through referenda. There is no need for money, and its economy is:

> ... so much a part of society that it is hardly worthy of a separate definition, and which is limited only by imagination, philosophy (and manners), and the idea of a minimally wasteful elegance; a kind of galactic ecological awareness allied to a desire to create beauty and goodness. (Banks, 1994: 4)

DOI: 10.1057/9781137436696.0004

Technology has created an existence of plenitude, and without material want there is little crime and no need for laws beyond 'agreed-on forms of behaviour' (Ibid.: 14). The end of capitalism brings also the end of exploitation:

> nobody in the Culture is exploited. It is essentially an automated civilisation in its manufacturing processes, with human labour restricted to something indistinguishable from play, or a hobby. (Ibid.: 5)

As resources are abundant, technology enables the most extravagant of whims to be indulged. Humans can control their own bodies and emotions through conscious manipulation of body-chemistry, and disease has effectively been banished:

> Thanks to that genetic manipulation, the average Culture human will be born whole and healthy and of significantly (though not immensely) greater intelligence than their basic human genetic inheritance might imply … the major changes … would include an optimised immune system and enhanced senses; freedom from inheritable diseases or defects, the ability … to fully recover from wounds which would either kill or permanently mutilate without such genetic tinkering. (Ibid.: 8)

Simultaneously, this technological wonderland is a sensuous and playful paradise. In a world where people can, and habitually do, change not only their sex repeatedly over a lifetime, but even change their species; Freudian taboos about sexual relations are redundant. The Culture is, in short, a 'secular heaven' (Banks in Jacobs, 2009).

While the aforementioned characteristics place Banks' projections within a familiar techno-scientific frame, they depart from previous iterations of this kind by the central role accorded to the non-human in envisioning utopia. The Culture comprises not only human (and humanoid) beings but also A.I.s of various descriptions. These silicon-based artificial intelligences (what Banks calls Minds) are embodied variously as sentient spaceships, huge space stations (Orbitals), small drones and android avatars. These Minds are the distant descendants of thinking machines created by humans, but have advanced to the point of possessing unfathomable levels of intelligence and insight – they are far more knowledgeable and powerful than their human or biological counterparts. Despite having evolved to the point of near-godhood, there is nothing tyrannical about Banks' Minds; they are scrupulously moral and act as humanity's guides, guardians and companions. The Culture is built

DOI: 10.1057/9781137436696.0004

around this 'pacific and mutually advantageous interaction between human beings and intelligent machines' (Roco and Bainbridge, quoted in Rumpala, 2011: 4). However powerful, the A.I.s are neither inscrutable nor emotionless, but instead they are possessed of distinctive individual personalities, complete with their own idiosyncratic quirks, interests and sense of humour (something Banks communicates through the kinds of names that Minds choose for themselves, such as *No More Mr Nice Guy*, *Screw Loose*, *Of Course I Still Love You*, *Little Rascal*, and *Kiss My Ass*). Indeed, Minds are amongst the most memorable of Banks' characters, the subjects of his narratives rather than mere objects that inhabit a human-centred future. In essence, Banks extrapolates from our current state of computational development to imagine a future in which benign sentient machines can resolve the seemingly intractable problems facing humanity today. As Lippens (2002: 136) suggests, Banks presents 'peace – utopian peace – as the product or outcome of specific *technological* cultures'. Far from a speculative fancy, Banks deems the development of such machine intelligences 'as not only likely in the future of our own species, but probably inevitable' (Banks, 1994: 4). Such assessments fall within a broader recent trend in thinking about technology, which holds that the rapid development of computational power will lead to a point of 'singularity' – at which super- and post-human intelligence will transform society beyond recognition. As mathematician, computer scientist and science fiction author Vernor Vinge (1993) puts it:

> we are on the edge of change comparable to the rise of human life on Earth. The precise cause of this change is the imminent creation by technology of entities with greater than human intelligence ... When greater-than-human intelligence drives progress, that progress will be much more rapid.

One of the scenarios that he postulates might produce the singularity that 'large computer networks (and their associated users) may "wake up" as a superhumanly intelligent entity' (Ibid.); in other words, the internet itself may evolve into a post-human intelligence that in turn will drive transformative progress. Pioneering A.I. researcher Ray Kurzweil has predicted that – extrapolation from the current pace of development – computers will exceed humans in intelligence by the year 2029 (Khomani, 2014).

Banks' themes of 'computational salvation', the imagining of a wholesale transformation of human society for the better through the development of A.I., is taken further in the Polity novels of Neal Asher. Starting with *Gridlinked* (2001) and elaborated through ten subsequent books, Asher imagines an interstellar human civilisation some 500 years from the present time. The starting point for his future history is distinctly dystopian – by the early 21st century humanity is on the brink of annihilation through a combination of war and ecological catastrophe. Salvation comes from an incremental take-over of Earth (a 'quiet revolution') by A.I.s, led by 'Earth Central'. Seeing that humans are unable or unwilling to address the urgent problems confronting them, the intelligent machines take it upon themselves to act. They go on to prove themselves much better fit for rule than humans, and create an advanced civilisation characterised by plenitude, longevity and human enhancement through genetic engineering and integration with computer technology. The malcontents of this future are a small group of anti-A.I. 'separatists' who perpetrate acts of mass murder in an attempt to overthrow the benign rule of the machine intelligences; many of the novels follow the exploits of Cormac, a human agent of the A.I.s, whose job it is to thwart these 'terrorists'. Secession from the Polity, and from the guidance of the A.I.s, ends not in the restoration of human autonomy and self-determination, but regression – one such world ends up as a religious theocracy (and is ultimately destroyed), and another rapidly collapses into tribal primitivism and seeks re-admittance to the Polity. In Asher's imaginary of the future, our path away from our self-destruction lies in the hands of our own creations, intelligent machines that will save humanity from its own worst inclinations and limitations.

The third author in whose work we can trace the shifting contours of techno-scientific utopianism is Isaac Asimov. His *Foundation* series of novels is particularly instructive given the long span over which it was produced, a span during which a significant shift takes place in the utopian cultural imaginary about science and technology. The first three volumes in the sequence (*Foundation, Foundation and Empire* and *Second Foundation*) were published between 1951 and 1953 (having previously been serialised in *Astounding Magazine* between 1941 and 1950). It was not until 1981 that the first of four further volumes in the series was published. Two of the later novels pick up events occurring after those depicted in the original trilogy, and another two are chronological prequels, covering events predating those described in the earlier books. In the writings of the 1940s and 1950s, technology appears as an adjunct or convenient facilitator of the human-centred story of scientific salvation that serves as their focus. In the terms used by Raymond Williams in

DOI: 10.1057/9781137436696.0004

his classification of utopian strands in science fiction, these novels are centred upon 'the willed transformation' of the world for the better by concerted human action and reason. However, in the books published 40 years later, intelligent machines appear as central characters and protagonists of the novels, in the form of sentient robots. *Prelude to Foundation* (1988) charts the life of Hari Seldon, Asimov's 'scientist-shaman', as a young man taking the first steps towards creating the science of psychohistory, whilst struggling to survive against the political plots and intrigues that bedevil the crumbling Empire. Yet psychohistory, the key to humankind's future, is re-presented alongside Seldon's own rise to prominence as the ultimate outcome of plans laid by sentient robots. The robots, created by humans in the distant past, have been forgotten in the mists of time, alongside the existence of mankind's original home planet, Earth. They have, nevertheless, main-tained their vigil over humanity across the aeons, led by the immortal R. Daneel Olivaw (the 'R' stands for 'Robot'), who sees the mission of himself and his kind as the protection and preservation of the human race. Seldon is befriended, assisted and protected by a young historian, Dors Venabili (who later becomes his wife); but Venabili is, in fact, one of Olivaw's fellow robots, sent by him to watch over Seldon and keep him safe as he develops his new predictive science. In Asimov's benign and comforting vision of artificial intelligences, their care and solici-tude towards humans (and humanity as a whole) is embedded in their very make-up. All such sentient machines are bound to obey the 'laws of robotics', whose ultimate basis (a kind of A.I. 'categorical imperative') is that 'a robot may not harm humanity, or, by inaction, allow humanity to come to harm' (Clarke, 1994). It is this law, iron-clad and central to the robots' self-definition and purpose, that propels them to secure the future of the human species.

Of the four authors considered here, William Gibson is perhaps anomalous, insofar as his projections of the hi-tech future clearly lack the optimism apparent in the works of Banks, Asimov and other techno-utopians. If anything, his vision of society is saturated with darkness. *Neuromancer* ([1984] 1995) and its sequels take place in the Sprawl, as a vast urban agglomeration characterised by extremes of wealth and poverty where crime and deviance are ubiquitous. His troubled pro-tagonists (burned-out hackers, addicts, mercenaries) struggle to survive in the space between murderous street gangs on the one hand, and the even-more deadly and amoral corporations that now rule the world for

DOI: 10.1057/9781137436696.0004

all intents and purposes. Gibson himself explicitly refuses to be situated within the distinction between utopian and dystopian:

> I don't think I'm dystopian at all. No more than I'm utopian. The dichotomy is hopelessly old-fashioned, really. What we have today is a combination of the two. (Gibson, quoted in Seed, 2003: 70)

Yet, with respect to his vision of the transcendent possibilities of cyberspace (a term he is credited with first coining), Gibson may be situated within the cadre of virtual utopians. The space of computerised interactions imagined in *Neuromancer* (which he dubs the Matrix) is all-encompassing and immersive, a world as intensive and extensive as any that might exist in the realm of the material:

> *A consensual hallucination* experienced daily by billions of legitimate operators, in every nation, by children being taught mathematical concepts ... A graphic representation of data abstracted from the bank of every computer in the human system. Unthinkable complexity. Lines of light ranged in the nonspace of the mind, clusters and constellations of data. (Gibson ([1984] 1995: 67)

Gibson's cyberspace is not simply a facsimile or digital reproduction of material reality. Rather, it is 'a place of rapture and erotic intensity, of powerful desire and even self-submission. In the Matrix, things attain a super-vivid hyper-reality. Ordinary experience seems dull and unreal by comparison' (Heim, 1993: 84). Cyberspace is depicted here as a kind of 'technological sublime' (Coyne, 2001: 63), and indeed takes on not only metaphysical but also theological overtones. This is most clearly apparent in *Neuromancer*'s account of the rise of A.I. in cyberspace; the culmination of the novel depicts the self-creation of a super-intelligent artificial being that now exists, entirely unintended and unanticipated, in the Matrix. This entity, Wintermute/Neuromancer, is in effect a digital god, the next stage in the evolution of consciousness. This theme of technological transcendence is continued in the sequels to *Neuromancer, Count Zero* (1986) and *Mona Lisa Overdrive* (1988), in which A.I.s become 'divine personages, complete with worshippers upon whom they shower benefits, including power, prestige and knowledge' (Geraci, 2007: 973).

The novels of Banks, Asher, Asimov and Gibson admittedly diverge widely in terms of style, structure and content. However, what brings them into convergence is the shared belief in the utopian possibilities that arise from the development of computational technology. At some

DOI: 10.1057/9781137436696.0004

point (perhaps very soon) the custodianship for humanity and its future will be passed along to the machine intelligences that we ourselves will create – and are, indeed, supposedly in the process of creating through digital technologies. The virtual utopianism found in such fictions finds its counterparts in a range of other contemporary discourses, especially those that focus upon the internet and its associated technologies and uses. These kinds of net-centric utopian constructions will provide the focus of discussion for the next chapter.

DOI: 10.1057/9781137436696.0004

3
Virtual Utopias and the Imaginary of the Internet

Abstract: *This chapter offers a detailed exploration of cultural representations of the internet as a utopian space in which self-identity, social relations and community life may be revitalised and reconfigured. In contrast with a 'disenchanted' and corrupted world of the 'real', the virtual promises liberation and renewal. Such constructions of virtual utopianism are explored through a critical reading of works by the likes of Sherry Turkle, Howard Rheingold, John Perry Barlow and Edward Castronova, alongside the language of internet evangelism and popular culture.*

Yar, Majid. *The Cultural Imaginary of the Internet: Virtual Utopias and Dystopias.* Basingstoke: Palgrave Macmillan, 2014. DOI: 10.1057/9781137436696.0005.

The preceding chapter explored techno-scientific utopianism across the discourses of social science and science fiction, and proposed that such projections have increasingly migrated to the realm of virtuality and cyberspace. The emergence of computers and artificial intelligence as themes in science fiction utopianism is, of course, intimately connected to the development of computerised communication technologies in recent decades. We need not rehearse in detail here the rise of computers in the home and workplace, or the phenomenal growth of computer-mediated communication and electronic environments such as the World Wide Web. Suffice it to say that these developments have been rapid, impacting manifold spheres of social life including work, commerce, leisure, politics, consumption and intimacy. Cultural discourse (spanning the genres of fiction, philosophy, politics, economics and so on) has from the outset speculatively projected such developments so as to imagine their consequences in terms of how they might reshape social relations across manifold spheres, and indeed may reshape the essential experience of 'being human' itself. This chapter will examine the varieties of 'virtual utopianism' that have coalesced around the internet. However, before doing so, it is necessary to reflect upon the deeper cultural roots of such discourses, roots that run deep in modernity's understanding of change and progress.

The discourse of virtual utopianism does not appear *ex nihilo*, nor is it configured simply in response to the experiences of recent techno-social change. Rather, it recuperates and re-inflects long-standing utopian imaginaries that are co-extensive with the experience of modernity. Indeed, we may suggest that philosophical modernism is itself fundamentally utopian (Kumar, 1991: 51). As Marshall Berman (1988: 15) eloquently articulates, the modernist ethos is founded upon the experience of perpetual change: 'To be modern is to find ourselves in an environment that promises adventure, power, joy, growth, transformation of ourselves and the world.' Yet this experience of change is given a powerful teleological character – the unmaking of the past and the creation of the future are linked to ideas of progress and human betterment. Virtual utopianism is, I would suggest, energised by this philosophical sensibility, seeing in technological change the blueprint of progress. However, the relationship between virtual utopianism and the modernist credo is rather more complex than it may appear at first. Richard Coyne (2001) characterises emergent narratives of the digital as forms of what he calls 'technoromanticism'. They synthesise in a new way two received modes of utopian thinking: the scientific rationalism of Enlightenment progress *and* the Romantic critique of modernity. From the former they borrow the hope that technology is the key to human self-improvement and social transformation – a conjoining of two notions of progress, the technological and the moral (Eder, 1990). From the latter, they take the aspiration for self-realisation and holism that is the hallmark of Romanticism. For technoromantic utopianism, the Romantic striving for imagination, creativity and unity is now to be realised not via a 'return to nature' or the 'organic' (recurrent themes of 19th-century Romantic literature and philosophy – McGann, 1985), but by embracing the technological and artificial. Thus, for example, the mind and imagination are set free to experience transcendence through immersion in the sphere of cyber-consciousness. Central to such imaginaries is an aspiration to restore human connection (and communion, unity) via technological mediation and synthesis, a connection that has supposedly been fractured and broken by the overly instrumental and rational use of technology (echoing the critiques of modern techno-science developed variously by Adorno and Horkheimer (1997) and Heidegger (1978)).

The rise of virtual utopianism can be understood as simultaneously both a continuation of Enlightenment modernity's ideology of progress-via-technology *and* an admission of that ideology's exhaustion. Insofar as the promise of progress has failed to deliver equality, solidarity, freedom, peace and self-realisation, the virtual serves as an alternative imaginary space in which such aspiration may be finally realised. Such utopian aspirations are articulated most clearly in the ideas of early internet evangelists such as John Perry Barlow. Barlow (a musician famous as part of the 1960s' counter-cultural icons *The Grateful Dead*, who went on to found the Electronic Frontier Foundation) published in 1996 his now famous 'A Declaration of the Independence of Cyberspace' (1996). He begins his 'declaration' (self-consciously echoing the clarion call of the American Declaration of Independence) thus:

> Governments of the Industrial World, you weary giants of flesh and steel, I come from Cyberspace, the new home of Mind. On behalf of the future, I ask you of the past to leave us alone. You are not welcome among us. You have no sovereignty where we gather.

The logic of Barlow's utopianism rests on an ontological distinction between the materiality of industrial society ('flesh and steel') and the 'new' realm of virtuality, a space of 'mind' not 'matter'. His rejection of

DOI: 10.1057/9781137436696.0005

the 'weary giants' bespeaks a final judgement on the supposed exhaustion of modernity's vision of material progress, and sets it against a new realm of possibility in which the old mechanisms of power, authority and control should have no sway. All of the social categories, individual and collective identities, and institutionalised order of the modern world are rejected in the most uncompromising terms:

> We are creating a world that all may enter without privilege or prejudice accorded by race, economic power, military force, or station of birth.
>
> We are creating a world where anyone, anywhere may express his or her beliefs, no matter how singular, without fear of being coerced into silence or conformity.
>
> Your legal concepts of property, expression, identity, movement, and context do not apply to us. They are all based on matter, and there is no matter here.

Barlow acknowledges that while our material embodiment consigns us to subjugation in the realm of materiality, our migration to the virtual promises rebirth in a realm of freedom that transcends the limitations of the reality left behind:

> We must declare our virtual selves immune to your sovereignty, even as we continue to consent to your rule over our bodies. We will spread ourselves across the Planet so that no one can arrest our thoughts ... We will create a civilization of the Mind in Cyberspace.

A similar faith in the transformative (indeed revolutionary) power of the internet was articulated by Barlow's fellow 1960s' counter-cultural guru, Timothy Leary. A Harvard psychologist, Leary became feted (and vilified) for his experiments with psychedelic drugs, which he believed held the key to transforming consciousness and treating psychiatric disorders (Stevens, 1988). By the 1980s, computers had replaced LSD as the cornerstone of his vision for a better, freer future – from exhorting people to 'turn on, tune in, and drop out' he went on to suggest that people should 'turn on, boot up, and jack in' to the new realm of cyberspace (Leary, 1994: 176). He believed that:

> We are...mutating into another species...we're moving into Cyberia. We are creatures crawling to the center of the cybernetic world...Never before has the individual been so empowered. (Ibid.: vii)

The likes of Barlow and Leary offer an extravagant vision of the technocentric future, in which the world (and humanity itself) will be renewed

DOI: 10.1057/9781137436696.0005

through the embrace of the digital. While other virtual utopians may not imagine the future in such flamboyant terms, they, nevertheless, converge upon the idea of redeeming the utopian promise of modernity through a turn to the virtual. Below I excavate and examine what I identify as the 'five modes of virtual utopianism' – cultural discourses focused upon the internet that envisage its capacity to transform society for the better across various domains of social life. These five modes relate to (1) the dream of democracy, (2) the rediscovery of community, (3) achieving equality, (4) the realisation of the self and (5) the transcendence of the human.

Five modes of virtual utopianism

The Dream of Democracy. Modernity's utopianism enjoys a deep and abiding affinity with the idea of democracy – the dream of a society in which autonomy is made possible through collective self-governance of the people, for the people and by the people. From the French Revolution's call for the overthrow of aristocratic and ecclesiastical authority to Tocqueville's vision of *Democracy in America* ([1835](2003)), political empowerment and formal equality in the practice of governance have played a central role in the imagining of modern utopias. At one level, we may suggest that the past few centuries have seen remarkable success in the realisation of democratic aspirations. More than half the world's countries are now deemed to be democracies (EIU, 2012), and the cumulative struggles of the labour movement, feminists and civil rights activists have helped extend the political franchise to all adult citizens. Yet there is an abiding sense across the 'advanced industrial world' that democracy is enduring a long-drawn out crisis of legitimacy. It is repeatedly stated that there is a 'democratic deficit' in which political institutions have become unresponsive to the citizenry, instead being captured by a self-serving political elite and/ or guided by the interests of corporate capitalism (Chomsky, 2006; Nabatchi, 2010). Survey findings repeatedly claim that public trust in governments and elected leaders is at an all-time low (Foremski, 2014), and that there is a pervasive sense of popular cynicism and disempowerment where politics is concerned. This sense of crisis (justified or otherwise) furnishes the backdrop against which virtual utopians imagine the internet as the avenue through which the malaise can be

DOI: 10.1057/9781137436696.0005

addressed, and by means of which a genuinely democratic society can be built.

Early advocates of digital democracy saw in the internet an inherent democratising logic. In *The Second Media Age* (1995) Mark Poster drew a clear distinction between 'old' and 'new' media. The mass media consolidated during the 19th and 20th centuries (print, radio, film and television) share significant structural features that organise users' engagements with them. First, they are characterised by a 'few-to-many' model of communication – a small number of media producers disseminate discourses to a mass audience, such that there are few 'speakers' and many more 'listeners'. Second, these mass media are organised into 'one way' channels – communication flows unidirectionally from producers to consumers, but seldom in the other direction. This few-to-many and one-way structure effectively limits and constrains societal interaction with mediated communication, such that the mass of people are the recipients but not the makers of such communication. In the political sphere, these communicative constraints serve to silence the majority, and equally serve to empower a small and select group who have the ability to control the flow of information and define reality through mass media representations (to borrow Althusser's (1994) classic terminology, the mass media serves as part of an 'ideological state apparatus'). For Poster and others, the development of the internet and WWW radically transform this scenario by empowering users, who are now enabled to generate and disseminate communication freely, by-passing the control of established mass media channels. The 'many' are now able to share information, ideas and opinions on a global scale, unconstrained by the limitations of geography or distance. This reshaping of the structure of mediated communication is seen as the fertile ground upon which a radical revival of democracy can take root:

> users ... have decentralized, distributed, direct control over when, what, why, and with whom they exchange information. That's the Internet model today, and it seems to breed critical thinking, activism, democracy, and quality. (Kapor, 1993)

Below we consider briefly three important ways that this political effervescence is envisaged.

First, internet-based communication is presented as a powerful mechanism for enhancing political accountability. This is based upon

DOI: 10.1057/9781137436696.0005

the amplification of *visibility* in the new media age. John Thompson (2005: 31) argues that digital communication technologies have created a 'new visibility' in which 'one no longer has to be present in the same spatial-temporal setting in order to see the other or to witness an action or event', including the actions of the politically powerful. This enhanced availability to the public gaze, combined with networked communications' capacity to transcend borders and evade mechanisms of editorial censorship, means that the actions (and inactions) of elected leaders cannot be kept secret, and the consequent public awareness of those actions enables citizens to demand and expect accountability. This logic of empowerment-through-visibility would appear to underpin initiatives such as Wikileaks. As the organisation itself proclaims:

> Publishing improves transparency, and this transparency creates a better society for all people. Better scrutiny leads to reduced corruption and stronger democracies in all society's institutions, including government, corporations and other organisations ... Scrutiny requires information ... We believe that it is not only the people of one country that keep their own government honest, but also the people of other countries who are watching that government through the media. (Wikileaks, 2014)

The possibilities identified with such endeavours have led commentators to conclude that, in the case of Wikileaks, 'A small, movement-based website has inflicted a tremendous informational defeat on the world's last superpower, revealing the possible emergence of a global networked counter-power able to mount effective resistance against the world-system' (Robinson and Karatzogianni, 2012).

The second dimension of virtual utopianism's hopes for democratic revival relates to a supposed capacity of the internet to facilitate popular participation in the political process. At one level popular opinion can impact upon decision-making through mechanisms such as online petitions (Grossman, 2000; Ward et al., 2003). It now seems almost obligatory for democratic states to institutionalise mechanisms through which citizens can petition for or against particular policy initiatives; at the time of writing, the UK government's e-petition website hosts more than 5,500 open petitions (HM Government, 2014). At a more systematic level, it has been suggested that the limitations and shortcomings of representative democracy may be by-passed via ICT-enabled 'direct democracy' through use of referenda, as well a form of 'deliberative democracy' through which all 'stakeholders' can impact upon public policy decisions

DOI: 10.1057/9781137436696.0005

(Dahlberg, 2001). As the American political commentator Dick Morris (2001: 1033–4) stated:

> The Internet offers a potential for direct democracy so profound that it may well transform not only our system of politics but also our very form of government ... The result will be a system of governance that pays closer heed to public views and that tethers more closely to the opinions of the people.

The third strand of political virtual utopianism focuses not upon the repair or reinvigoration of existing political systems and institutions, but upon their revolutionary overthrow. In their widely discussed book *Empire* (2001) Michael Hardt and Antonio Negri argue that the contemporary world is dominated by a new kind of imperial power, one built around the global domination of capital and its associated institutions. However, they hold that resistance to Empire is not only possible but in a sense inevitable; new communication technologies, which have played a key role in securing the new hegemony, are themselves appropriated 'into a weapon of liberation from these oppressive forces' (Miller, 2011: 156). This resistance comes not from the traditional collective revolutionary subjects of modernity (the proletariat, national liberation movements or organised political parties) but from something much more immanent, elemental and inchoate – a spontaneous coalescence of 'atoms' that Hardt and Negri dub the 'multitude' (Tampio, 2009: 387); 'the multitude ... consists in the possibility of directing technologies ... towards its own joy and its own increase of power' (Hardt and Negri, 2001: 396). We may suggest here that this combination of technological appropriation and vital affective energy is quintessentially 'technoromantic' in the terms set out by Coyne (2001). This notion of a global network of radical political action, united through the mediating capacities of new communication technologies, has of late been used to claim an upsurge of resistance to hegemonic power (see, for example, Fenton, 2008). In particular, the events of the so-called Arab Spring have been identified as exemplars of a new politics of revolution that depends centrally upon the internet and related ICTs. The term 'Arab Spring' is now commonly used to denote a number of broad-based social movements for reform across North Africa and the Middle East that gained rapid momentum from early 2011, as well as earlier mass mobilisations that occurred in 2009. These movements (sometimes co-mingled with armed insurrection) led to the collapse of autocratic regimes in Tunisia, Egypt, Yemen and Libya, and have also manifested in popular mobilisations in Iran, Bahrain, Syria,

DOI: 10.1057/9781137436696.0005

Kuwait, Oman, Lebanon, Morocco and Jordan. The uprisings in Tunisia and Egypt featured a significant use of the internet (especially social media platforms such as Facebook and Twitter) in mobilising support, organising demonstrations and disseminating information via alternatives to official state-censored media (Chokoshvili, 2011; Stepanova, 2011; Hassan, 2012). Such is the significance popularly attached to ICTs in these events that they have been dubbed 'Facebook revolutions' and 'Twitter revolutions'. Former US national security advisor Mark Pfeifle accorded such importance to new media channels in the unfolding events that he suggested Twitter be nominated for the Nobel Peace Prize (Khan, 2009). For political techno-utopians, it would appear that even if 'the revolution will not be televised', it certainly will be Tweeted, re-Tweeted, re-posted, shared and 'liked'.

The Rediscovery of Community. From the late medieval to the early modern period, a powerful trading alliance arose in northern Europe in the form of the Hanseatic free cities. Inscribed above the gates of many of these cities was the motto *Stadtluft macht frei* – 'city air makes one free' (Smith, 2012: 219). These words in many ways exemplify the intimate connection between modernist utopianism and the *topos* of the city. From Plato's *kallipolis* onwards, the city has long featured as the site and space of utopian existence (Mumford, 1922), yet for modernists it becomes indispensable. The city stands for all that modernity affords in the name of progress, in contrast to the country which denotes the shackles of tradition and stasis:

> On the city has gathered the idea of an achieved centre: of learning, communication, light … on the country as a place of backwardness, ignorance, limitation. (Williams, 1973: 1)

Modern science, industry and engineering would build the city as a monument to reason and order, and in doing so distribute 'the benefits of the Machine Age to all and [direct] the community onto the paths of social harmony' (Fishman, 1982: 4). To borrow Le Corbusier's famous phrase, such cities would become 'machines for living'. However, over the past 50 years, the cultural figuration of the city has undergone a dramatic reversal, and has become indelibly associated not with the dream of techno-scientific progress but with the nightmare of its failure (Baeten, 2010). The city is now imagined as a space of dysfunction, division, exclusion, separation, alienation and incivility; it has become something of a leitmotif for all that is supposedly missing from modern

DOI: 10.1057/9781137436696.0005

life – community, solidarity, intimacy, connection, reciprocity. Cities are now places characterised by 'endemic forms of urban alienation and the disappearance or non-existence of urban neighbourhood community identity' (Foth and Adkins, 2006). This sensibility lays the foundations for virtual utopianism's hopes for a revival of community, either through a technological reinvention of the city itself, or through its transcendence in the realm of cyberspace.

In *Smart Cities: Big Data, Civic Hackers and the Quest for a New Utopia* (2013), Anthony Townsend imagines a city reinvented and revitalised through digitisation. 'Smart cities' he suggests 'are places where information technology is wielded to address problems old and new... We are witnessing the birth of a new civic movement' (xii, xiv). The key driver of this renewal is the power ICTs afford to foster human connectedness and revive the social bonds and relations of everyday reciprocity and co-operation that have been in terribly short supply in the anonymous environment of the modern city:

> we're learning new ways to thrive on mass connectedness. A sharing economy has mushroomed overnight, as people swap everything from spare bedrooms to cars, in a synergistic exploitation of new technology. (Ibid.: 16)

The hope is that electronic mediation will 'create the richness of interaction... lacking in modern communities ... they [will] enable urban sociability' (Ibid.: 143, 160). A perfect illustrative example is offered by a 2004 report in the *New York Times*. It relates how student Mohit Santram chose to share his Wi-Fi connection with anyone in the vicinity of his East Village apartment. However, those 'picking up his signal are first directed to a bulletin board where they can post and read neighborhood information and gossip' (Keldoulis, 2004). Santram is a participant in Neighbournode, a peer-to-peer application that facilitates online interaction between people living in proximity to one another:

> with a Neighbornode you can broadcast a message to roughly everyone whose apartment window is within 300 feet of yours (and has line of sight), and they can broadcast messages back to you... Additionally, Neighbornodes are linked together, making up a node network to enable the passing of news and information on a street-by-street basis throughout the wider community. (P2P Foundation, 2009)

The initiative aims 'to let communities of otherwise anonymous urbanites find one another' (Keldoulis, 2004), thereby rebuilding locally

DOI: 10.1057/9781137436696.0005

based community identity and its associated relations of reciprocal exchange.

While these aforementioned strands of virtual utopianism gesture towards the renewal of place-based social bonds, the dominant trend has been towards imagining the creation of new forms of community that exist purely or predominantly in the cyber-sphere. In an early considera-tion of virtual communities, Howard Rheingold (1993) postulated that spaces of online interaction (such as forums, chatrooms and bulletin boards) point the way for a rediscovery of human inter-connectedness and solidarity. As Miller (2011: 191) notes, Rheingold's starting point is an assessment of contemporary urban (and suburban) life as increasingly denuded of possibilities for social exchange and collective engagement. Echoing influential critiques of contemporary Western societies by the likes of Fukuyama (1996) and Putnam (2000), Rheingold sees a yearning for recreating everyday civic engagements that can be satisfied in the vir-tual realm. The bonds and connections formed online serve a multitude of valuable purposes, ranging from exchange of news and knowledge, collaborative working, through leisure and recreation, to therapy and friendship. Moreover, online communities (unlike offline communities based around residential proximity) enable individuals to connect with others who share with them common interests, goals, aspirations, values and passions. They also address the disruption to human relationships that arise from ever-increasing levels of geographical mobility (Miller, 2011: 192), as well as helping those suffering from ill-health and dis-ability to overcome isolation (Foley, 2004). More recent spaces of online interaction, such as social networking sites, have been claimed to offer numerous positive outcomes for their users, including an accumulation of social capital, improved psychological well-being and overcoming low self-esteem (Valkenburg et al., 2006; Ellision et al., 2007; Park et al., 2009). Raine and Wellman (2012) see digital facilitation of this kind supporting the emergence of a new 'networked individualism' that will become the basis of negotiating friendship, support, advice and mutual assistance in the future.

Achieving Equality. The development of industrial capitalism was marked by tremendous gains in economic productivity, with modern societies experiencing 'high growth rates, steadily rising per capita incomes, and technological change' (Goldstone, 2002: 324). Yet, dur-ing this span of time, the gaps between rich and poor have continued to expand; by 2013, some 46 per cent of the world's wealth lay in the

DOI: 10.1057/9781137436696.0005

hands of 1 per cent of its population (Puzzanghera, 2014). Such patterns of growing income inequality are apparent both *between* developed and developing countries, and *within* advanced economies such as the US (where income inequality is now said to be at its highest level since the 1920s – Desilver, 2013). The explanations for this trend are complex and contested, but one influential line of argument is that the gradual transformation of advanced economies from an industrial to post-industrial basis has marginalised those at the lower ends of the socio-economic structure (Hout et al., 1993). In the so-called knowledge economies, access to advanced education and skills is a prerequisite for securing well-remunerated employment, a situation which exacerbates divisions between the upper and lower reaches of the class structure and entrenches inequality (Gershuny, 1993; Rohrbach, 2009). In the information economy, there is a polarisation between highly educated and highly skilled knowledge workers on the one hand, and low-waged service workers on the other; the latter are not only poorly remunerated but also suffer insecurity in terms of employment stability. Insofar as the development of ICTs has been a central driver in the emergence of this new economy (Bell, 1976; Toffler, 1980), they appear clearly implicated in entrenching problems of inequality and exclusion:

> Middle class households can offer their children access to powerful new learning opportunities, such as computers and on line services, which families of poorer children cannot dream of affording. (Perelman, 1988: 9)

This so-called digital divide (Loader, 1998; Mossberger et al., 2003) has been seized upon by those sceptical of claims made about the socially benign effects of the digital revolution (Webster, 2006: 146–50). However, virtual utopians see in the internet the means to challenge and ameliorate economic inequalities, providing unprecedented opportunities for participation in the knowledge society for the heretofore socially marginalised. The prospect of universal and free virtual access to knowledge, information and education is presented as the key to unlocking opportunity and promoting inclusion.

In his novel *The Diamond Age: Or, a Young Lady's Illustrated Primer* (1995), science fiction author Neal Stephenson provides an imaginative scenario about the power of ICTs to counter patterns of socio-economic inequality. The novel is set in a near future where nation states have been largely displaced by sovereign ethno-cultural tribes or 'phyles', each of which maintains self-contained enclaves organised according to

DOI: 10.1057/9781137436696.0005

shared cultural, moral and religious commitments. The story unfolds in and around the Neo-Victorian tribe of New Atlantis, a collective self-consciously styled around the values associated with Anglo-Saxon Victorian life (rectitude, decorum, hierarchy, patriarchal authority, respect for tradition and so on); despite its apparent anachronism, the tribe, in fact, depends upon a discrete but intensive use of new technologies. Like the Victorian world depicted by Dickens, this Neo-Victorian society of the future is marked by extremes of wealth and poverty, with a class of *thetes* (those denied tribal membership) eking-out a hand-to-mouth existence in slums. The story follows a young slum-dweller, Nell, whose social fate is transformed through access to technology when she becomes the unintended owner of a sophisticated, interactive electronic book, the *Young Lady's Illustrated Primer*. The device, originally created for the grandchild of a wealthy and powerful Neo-Victorian industrialist, is intended to impart the knowledge and skills a privileged young woman will need to take her place amongst the social elite. In the hands of an illiterate child of the lowest social orders, the book has a transformative effect upon Nell who through its tutelage grows into an educated and self-confident woman, and a leader in her own right. The novel is in essence a *bildungsroman* for the information age, gesturing towards the power of electronic technologies to liberate those who have been consigned to the margins of society through a lack of access to knowledge and education. The utopian hopes attached to the internet follow this template in imagining progressive social change arising from its supposed ability to disperse knowledge across the barriers of class, culture and nation:

> This communications revolution...has...enhanced the ability of less developed countries to tap into the global knowledge pool. The Internet is proving to be a tool of immense power in sharing knowledge...Today a child anywhere in the world who has Internet access has access to more knowledge than a child in the best schools of industrial countries did a quarter century ago. He or she is no longer isolated. (Stiglitz, 1999: 318)

> Imagine a network that spans the world. A network that delivers – invisibly and inexpensively – the myriad bits of information that will be the key to prosperity in the 21st century. Imagine a network that links...students with teachers ... This network, of course, is the Internet. (Spar, 1999: 344)

Such assessments have driven initiatives to expand and extend internet access – the supposed key to inclusion, social mobility and prosperity in a knowledge-driven world. In 2005, architect and technology enthusiast Nicholas Negroponte launched the One Laptop Per Child (OLPC) project, which aims to provide affordable mobile computing and internet access for children in the world's least-developed countries; it's self-styled 'mission is to empower the world's poorest children through education' (OLPC, 2014). In 2013, Google launched its Project Loon, which uses giant helium balloons to beam-in free Wi-Fi internet access to poor populations in the southern hemisphere (Kang, 2013). In 2014, Facebook founder Mark Zuckerberg announced an initiative aimed at extending internet access to the two-thirds of the global population who do not yet have it. He presents the importance of the project in the following terms:

> The internet... is... the foundation of the global knowledge economy... a knowledge economy encourages worldwide prosperity... By bringing everyone online, we'll... improve billions of lives. (Zuckerberg, 2014: 2–3)

The unwavering faith that the internet is the answer to problems of entrenched socio-economic inequality is also manifest in the recent explosion of interest in the so-called MOOC (Massive Open Online Learning) initiatives. A development of earlier distance-learning programmes, and centred upon online communication, the first MOOCs were launched at US universities such as Stanford and MIT around 2009 (Friedman, 2013; Lane, 2013). In the years since they have become the latest fashion in higher education; current estimates suggest that more than 200 universities worldwide provide MOOCs, offering more than 1200 courses taken by ten million students (Shah, 2013). MOOCs are intended to offer open access, free for users worldwide, to university-level courses across the sciences, arts and humanities. Internet enthusiasts have embraced MOOCs with near-evangelical zeal:

> there is one big thing happening that leaves me incredibly hopeful about the future, and that is the budding revolution in global online higher education. Nothing has more potential to lift more people out of poverty – by providing them an affordable education... Nothing has more potential to unlock a billion brains to solve the world's biggest problems. (Friedman, 2013)

Their proponents emphasise how the courses offer access to learning opportunities, at the world's leading universities, for those who would otherwise have no chance to benefit from such provision:

> For example, the 7,200 students who completed ... [the] ... MOOC in spring 2012 included an 81-year old man, a single mother with two children, and

DOI: 10.1057/9781137436696.0005

a 15-year old prodigy from Mongolia who got a perfect score on the final exam. (Waldrop, 2013)

Such is the belief in the internet's capacity to revolutionise access to education that some proponents of MOOCs (such as Stanford Professor of A.I., Sebastian Thrun) have already proclaimed the imminent death of the traditional 'bricks and mortar' university and the practice of face-to-face instruction:

> Having done this ... I feel like there's a red pill and a blue pill, and you can take the blue pill and go back to your classroom and lecture your 20 students. But I've taken the red pill, and I've seen Wonderland. (Thrun, quoted in Lewin, 2012)

In the new 'wonderland' of the internet, knowledge and opportunity for all will become the new norm.

The Realisation of the Self. There is no notion more modern than 'the idea that we construct our own social identity' (Hollis, 1985: 230). The imperative that we can, and should, be free to determine who we are is grounded in a revolution that places the self at the centre of the world. The newly minted category of the autonomous subject is accorded the power not only to apprehend truth, but to use that knowledge to shape itself and the world around it. Self-determination, unconstrained by the bonds of tradition, prejudice or hierarchy, is the right accorded to all by virtue of being human. The birth of the modern self sets in train a process of individualisation in which persons are both entitled and encouraged towards autonomous self-creation (Giddens, 1991; Beck and Beck-Gernsheim, 2001). Today, this 'reflexive project of the self' takes shape through myriad social and cultural practices through which identity work is performed and by means of which we claim recognition and esteem. Yet, as numerous scholars and critics have noted, this promise of freedom yields some perverse and unwelcome outcomes. On the one hand, autonomous self-creation takes on the character of an institutionalised compulsion, and life becomes configured as a struggle against impermanence and instability (Beck and Beck-Gernsheim, 1995; Honneth, 2004; Bauman, 2005). On the other hand, the ongoing hold of hierarchical and discriminatory cultural categories (such as those around gender, class, ethnicity, sexuality and disability) constrain individuals' capacities for self-realisation and social acceptance. As with modern societies' difficulties in realising hopes for democracy, community and equality, the dissatisfactions centred upon the project of

DOI: 10.1057/9781137436696.0005

self-realisation incite virtual utopians to look to the internet as a source of redemption.

In 1993, *The New Yorker* published a cartoon by Peter Steiner that depicts two canines; one is seated in front of a computer, paws on the keyboard, as it looks down and speaks to its companion. The caption accompanying the image states: 'On the Internet, nobody knows you're a dog.' Despite its humorous irreverence, this cartoon perhaps encapsulates the hopes bound-up with the internet in terms of its possibilities for facilitating self-realisation. As Nakamura (2001: 226–7) puts it, the cartoon suggests that:

> it is possible to ... represent yourself as a different gender, age, race, etc ... The freedom which the dog chooses to avail itself of is the freedom to 'pass' as part of a privileged group.

Early explorations of internet users' online engagements stressed the medium's capacity for facilitating the creation and expression of multiple self-identities. For example, in her influential study of Multi-User Domains (MUDs), Sherry Turkle (1997) examined how participants were empowered to creatively construct selves, adopting personas through which they could express the many and varied aspects of their identities. As one of Turkle's interviewees enthused:

> You can be whoever you want to be. You can completely redefine yourself if you want ... You can just be whoever you want, really, whoever you have the capacity to be ... It's easier to change the way people perceive you ... They don't look at your body and make assumptions. They don't hear your accent and make assumptions. All they see is your words. (quoted in Miller, 2011: 162)

Ideas about online identity construction have more recently been extended beyond the text-based interactions afforded by platforms such as MUDs to include more sophisticated virtual environments and digital simulations. The so-called Massively Multiplayer Online Role Playing Games (MMORPGs) offer users the opportunity to interact with others via virtual personae (avatars) in an immersive online world. One study of identity work in MMORPGs (Bessière et al., 2007) suggests that they enable participants to create and sustain online identities that are imbued with more favourable social characteristics than the individuals' attribute to themselves in the offline world. The authors claim that endowing virtual personae with favourable characteristics was more common

DOI: 10.1057/9781137436696.0005

amongst those with 'lower psychological well-being', and conclude that 'the game world allows players the freedom to create successful virtual selves regardless of the constraints of their actual situation' (Ibid.: 530). In other words, for those who find themselves unable to sustain a real-world self that enjoys recognition and affirmation, the virtual domain offers a valuable space for self-realisation.

In his book *Exodus to the Virtual World* (2007), Edward Castronova argues that the lure of virtual environments (what he calls 'synthetic worlds') will exercise an irresistible pull that will draw people in their millions away from the real world. For Castronova, 'the move to online goes hand in hand with the fullest possible expression of self', and therein lies the powerful attraction of the virtual. These worlds will become as complex, sophisticated and multi-faceted as the material realm, complete with social organisation, economic activity, political processes, and the activities of work, leisure, love and sex. He describes such worlds as a 'refuge' and an 'escape' from a reality that offers little in the way of 'moment to moment happiness' (192), reward or self-esteem for many people:

> if it's a heavy-set girl from a small town who gets victimised just because her body isn't the 'right' kind of body, and she goes online to make friends because she can't get a fair shake in the real world, then I would say the virtual world is ... a refuge. (Castronova, quoted in BBC News, 2007)

In the face of real-world circumstances that curtail and constrain many people's possibilities for self-realisation, the virtual becomes the perfect space in which authenticity, esteem and happiness can be experienced.

The Transcendence of the Human. Historical evidence suggests that pre-modern Europeans could have expected to live on average anywhere between 25 and 35 years (Riley, 2001: 32–3); today, this figure stands at 78.5 years (OECD, 2012). This dramatic shift can be attributed to a range of factors including improved diet as a result of agricultural mechanisation, better hygiene and sanitation and the interventions of modern medicine aimed at preventing, treating and curing diseases. Techno-scientific modernity promises a human life that is not only better (more free, satisfying, fulfilling), but longer; life will be good, and we will have more of it. Science provides the means to better understand the working of human biology, and technology (from pharmaceutical synthesis to diagnostic and surgical tools) furnishes the means for intervention in the name of greater human health and longevity. Technology is now

DOI: 10.1057/9781137436696.0005

used not only to act upon the human body, but also integrated within it so as to rectify problems and enhance its performance and resilience. Commonplace examples of such human–technological couplings include the implantation of artificial joints to replace those that have atrophied; pacemakers to regulate heart rhythms; cochlear implants to enable the profoundly deaf to hear; and retinal prostheses to restore vision. Such is the trend towards integrating the biological and mechanical, the human and the technological, that the figure of the 'cyborg' (a cybernetic organism) appears to have moved from the realms of fiction to everyday fact (Becker, 2000; Clarke, 2004). Virtual utopianism embraces the possibilities held out by such developments and projects a future in which the human will be transformed, and the inherent limitations dictated by our evolutionary heritage will be overcome.

The enhancement of the human mind and body with ICT so as to extend and multiply its capacities is, as noted in Chapter 2, a recurrent theme in techno-utopian science fiction. In Gibson's *Neuromancer* an art dealer gains a decisive advantage over his rivals by having a neural socket into which information chips can be inserted, giving him an instantaneous and encyclopedic knowledge of the market. In Neal Asher's *Polity* novels, it is commonplace for individuals to have a small augmentation device surgically wired into the brain, which offers direct access to the Net with just a thought; information is directly projected into the user's field of vision, where it can be explored and manipulated. In the TV series *Chuck* (2007–2012), a down-on-his-luck computer 'nerd' is transformed into a 'super spy' when a secret database called the Intersect is directly downloaded into his brain; the technology enables him not only to access a wealth of knowledge, but also to instantly call upon any skills he might need, ranging from disarming a bomb, flying a helicopter, speaking a foreign language, to a mastery of unarmed combat. At one level, this scenario simply reinvents the familiar fantasy of empowerment that turns a 'loser' into a superhero (Phillips and Strobl, 2013); yet it is telling that the mechanism of transformation is no longer exposure to 'cosmic rays', being bitten by a 'radioactive spider', or 'genetic mutation', but the power of information technology to 'rewire' the human brain. Recent developments in ICT likewise seek to realise the vision of enhancement via human–computer integration. For example, Google's 'Glass' project aims to bring to market a wearable device (resembling an ordinary pair of spectacles) which allows internet access via language commands, and which projects information into the user's field of vision, overlaying the

DOI: 10.1057/9781137436696.0005

world with a digital enhancement. As one technology commentator suggests:

> it is only a matter of time before Google Glass-type devices take the form of mechanisms that are physically incorporated into our bodies much in the same manner as glasses evolved into contact lenses... Google Glass may be the beginning of the final stage before intake and synthesis of information is done within our own bodies. (Goldring, 2013)

Beyond imagining the enhancement of humanity via cyber-technology, utopianism projects a transcendence of the most fundamental limitation upon our existence, namely our mortality. It is perhaps fair to suggest that the problem of human finitude is central to all philosophical, religious and cultural systems of thought; in Heidegger's (1977: 272) terms, our being is a being-towards-death (*Sein zum Tode*), and our existence is conditioned by an awareness of the inevitability of our own demise. However, for virtual utopians, the development of technology offers a pathway to exceed the constraints of mortality. A.I. expert and futurologist Ray Kurzweil holds that the integration of intelligent machines with human biology in the form of nanotechnology will soon make immortality a reality:

> We'll get to a point about 15 years from now where we're adding more than a year every year to your life expectancy... by the 2030s we'll be putting millions of nanobots inside our bodies to augment our immune system, to basically wipe out disease. (Kurzweil, in Goldman, 2013)

Such is Kurzweil's conviction that immortality is just around the corner, the 65 year-old reportedly consumes some 150 vitamin supplements daily, hoping to maintain his existence just long enough until the nanotechnology will enable him to live indefinitely (Kurzweil and Grossman, 2005; Lunau, 2013).

If the likes of Kurzweil envisage computer-powered technologies sustaining our bodily existence for potentially unlimited spans, other virtual utopians seek to dispense with the encumbrance of the flesh altogether. In 2011, multi-millionaire entrepreneur Dmitry Itskov established the '2045 Initiative', a non-profit organisation which aims to develop the technology necessary to transfer human consciousness into an computerised host in the coming decades. Amongst the goals Itskov has set is:

> to develop... technologies for moving the individual mind of the human being to a non-biological substrate – an artificial body... [which will] ... eliminate aging, illnesses and death. (Itskov, 2012)

DOI: 10.1057/9781137436696.0005

This realisation of what he calls 'neo-humanity' will:

> change the bodily nature of the human being, and make them immortal, free, playful, independent of limitations of space and time. These transformations will not restrict the individuality and freedom of each separate person, but on the contrary will ensure maximum creative development and reveal their unlimited potential. (Ibid.)

To recall the title of one of Wells' utopian fictions, the ultimate dream of virtual utopianism is to transform 'mere men' into something akin to digital gods.

*   *   *

In this chapter we have explored the different paths along which virtual utopianism projects a future existence in which the dream of progress, freedom and human self-realisation can be made real through the embrace of computer technology. This imaginary, I have suggested, recuperates modernity's faith in techno-science, while re-inscribing it into the space of the virtual. In the next chapter, we turn to examine the countervailing tendency in cultural discourse, that which renders techno-scientific change in distinctly dystopian terms.

DOI: 10.1057/9781137436696.0005

4

The Dystopian Worlds of Techno-Science

Abstract: *This chapter explores the dystopian cultural construction of science and technology across the discourses of social science, science fiction and popular film. This powerful language of disenchantment borrows heavily from Romantic critiques of modern society, and articulates wider cultural sensibilities about the dissolution of social order and stability in the modern world, alongside fears about the effects of technology as a force for dehumanisation and domination.*

Yar, Majid. *The Cultural Imaginary of the Internet: Virtual Utopias and Dystopias.* Basingstoke: Palgrave Macmillan, 2014. DOI: 10.1057/9781137436696.0006.

Romanticism, social science and modernity

If there is a key to understanding the dystopian imaginary of techno-scientific modernity, it lies in the cultural coordinates of Romanticism. As Michael Löwy and Robert Sayre (2001) note, the term itself is notoriously difficult to define, for a number of reasons. First, it has been used to denote a wide variety of cultural discourses, spanning novels, poetry, painting, music, philosophy, history, theology, sociology, political ideology and so on. Second, the traits or characteristics identified as hallmarks of Romanticism are extremely wide-ranging (including the valorisation of imagination, nature, myth, symbol and emotions). Third, Romanticism appears to be contradictory, in that it manifests in forms:

> simultaneously…revolutionary and counterrevolutionary, individualistic and communitarian, cosmopolitan and nationalist, realist and fantastic, retrograde and utopian, rebellious and melancholic, democratic and aristocratic. (Ibid.: 1)

However, underlying this complexity and heterogeneity, Löwy and Sayre identify a common worldview (*Weltanschauung*) which is centred upon 'the deeply antagonistic relations between Romanticism and industrial society' (Ibid.: 9):

> the common axis, the unifying elements of the Romantic movement in most if not all its manifestations across the principal centres in Europe…is opposition to the modern bourgeois world…Romanticism represents a critique of modernity…in the name of values and ideals drawn from the past. (Ibid.: 10, 17)

The Romantic revolt against modernity takes shape through a series of dualisms that juxtapose supposed essential human values against their attrition in the modern world of industrial society: unity versus disunity, collectivism versus individualism, isolation versus belonging, the emotions versus rationality, freedom versus control, the natural versus the artificial, flesh versus the machine, faith versus science and so on. Below we shall briefly examine three important figures in the development of social thought, all of whom inflect the Romantic worldview in a critique of techno-scientific modernity – Ferdinand Tönnies, Max Weber and Theodore Adorno.

Tönnies is best remembered as a foundational figure in 19th-century sociology, making substantial contributions to the development of both

DOI: 10.1057/9781137436696.0006

theory and method. Like his counterparts in England (Herbert Spencer) and France (Auguste Comte, Emile Durkheim) he sought to develop a system of classifications that could capture the profound changes in social organisation ushered in by industrial modernity. However, unlike the positivists, he did not view such change in terms of an evolutionary progression towards a better society; rather, influenced by the neo-Romanticism that flourished in Germany in the latter half of the 19th century (Trentmann, 1994: 592; Harris, 2001: xiv), he articulated a profound disquiet about the ongoing reordering of social life. His protestations that he offered merely objective descriptions of social change are undermined by an unmistakeable evaluative stance (Löwy and Sayre, 2001: 71). From his earliest and best-known work *Community and Society* (1887[2003]) to his last *Geist der Neuzeit* ([1935]2010) (*The Spirit of Modern Times*) his work is characterised by a mournful sense of loss in the face of modernity's world made anew:

> In the Middle Ages there was unity, now there is atomization ... then there was relative peace, now wars are wholesale slaughter; then there were sympathetic relationships amongst kinsfolk and old acquaintances, now there are strangers and aliens everywhere ... then there was permanency of abode, now great mobility; then there were folk arts, music and handicrafts, now there is science – and the scientific method applied ... leads to the point of view which deprives one's fellow men and one's society of their personality, leaving only a framework of dead symbols and generalizations. (Tönnies, in Loomis and McKinney, 2003: 2)

Tönnies' contemporary Max Weber similarly offers a tragic vision of the human consequences of modernisation. Weber is at one level a thorough Rationalist, something evident in his commitment to Neo-Kantianism. For Weber, human action must be grasped as an exercise of freedom that is shaped by subjects' sense-making activity, and that activity is itself amenable to scientific study via a rigorous and formal method (Koch, 1993: 123–4; Mackinnon, 2001: 334–6). However, the substantive analysis of society that emerges from this exercise of reason is profoundly shaped by a Romantic sensibility. Especially important is the *Sturm und Drang* (Storm and Stress) school of early German Romanticism, associated with the likes of Goethe and Schiller, with its emphasis upon the deadening separation of Man from Nature brought about the 'mechanised' world view of the Enlightenment (Koch, 1993: 126), and the destructive effects of blindly pursuing the scientific

DOI: 10.1057/9781137436696.0006

promise of development and progress. This is nowhere more eloquently articulated than in Goethe's *Faust*, where the price for the emerging industrial age is the unleashing of 'dark and fearful energies that may erupt with a horrible force beyond all human control' (Berman, 1988: 40). Likewise, in Weber's analysis of modern society, the seemingly unstoppable march of scientific reason yields not the freedom promised by Kant, but its opposite – the reduction of human subjects into objects of calculation and manipulation:

> it means that... one can, in principle, master all things by calculation. This means that the world is disenchanted... The fate of our times is characterized by rationalization and ... above all, by the 'disenchantment of the world.' Precisely the ultimate and most sublime values have retreated from public life. (Weber, 1991: 139, 156)

For Weber, modern science is more than a body of knowledge, a set of procedures for generating that knowledge, or its practical application in the form of tools and techniques. Rather, it is an all-encompassing world-view that defines and crucially narrows human existence and experience. This techno-scientific outlook drives the dynamic of disenchantment – it alienates humans from nature by turning the latter into dead matter that can be processed (Weber, 2005: 27); it inculcates a way of thinking that reduces human action to instrumental calculation (Maley, 2013); and ultimately subjects human life to a logic of control in the name of order, efficiency and productivity.

The critique of Enlightenment reason, science and technology developed by Weber finds its most forceful and concerted articulation in the work of Theodore Adorno and his Frankfurt School colleagues. In *The Dialectic of Enlightenment* ([1947]1997), neo-Marxists Adorno and Horkheimer decisively set themselves against Marx's own view of science and technology as progressive forces (Pippin, 1995: 49). Instead, the Enlightenment's elevation of scientific reason to the apex of human endeavour ultimately yields the very opposite of freedom and self-realisation – a totalising domination across all domains of social, political, cultural and economic life. The 'repressive technological nightmares' (Jay, 1996: 259) unleashed in modern society cannot be attributed to the misuse or abuse of techno-science under capitalism, but is inherent in scientific reason's logic of objectification and reification. In short, technology alienates men from each other and from themselves, stripping away the moral and aesthetic capacities that make us fully human:

> Technology is making gestures precise and brutal, and with them men. It expels from movement all hesitation, deliberation, civility... which driver is not tempted, merely by the power of his engine, to wipe out the vermin of the street, pedestrians, children and cyclists? The movements machines demand of their users already have the violent, hard-hitting, unresting jerkiness of Fascist maltreatment. (Adorno in Wiggershaus, 1995: 511)

This narrative of technological development is recuperated in the work of Marcuse, who sees in it the consolidation of a 'totally administered society' in which life is reduced to a banal and superficial 'one dimensionality'; 'The liberating force of technology – the instrumentalization of things – turns into a fetter of liberation; the instrumentalization of man' (Marcuse, [1964]2007: 163; see also discussion in Feenberg, 1996). Human beings' alienation from themselves and each other is mirrored, in a quintessentially Romantic assessment, by our alienation from nature; in the words of Ernst Bloch, technology 'stands in nature like an army of occupation in enemy territory' (Bloch in Löwy and Sayre, 2001: 181). The critique of technology developed by the likes of Weber and Adorno, in the shadow of Romanticism, has decisively shaped a dystopian outlook in social thought that reads the history of modernity as a tragedy of rationalisation, dehumanisation and domination (see, for example, Baudrillard, 1975; Winner, 1977; Bauman, 1989; Ellul, 2005; Virilio, 2012).

Across these varied dystopian assessments of modernity, we may suggest that technology is conceptualised in one of four (distinct but often inter-related) ways. First, it can be viewed as an *imperative*: it reverses the subject–object relation between humans and 'mere things', and the latter comes to dominate and direct the former. Second, it is viewed as a form of *reification*: it makes human being into something 'thing-like', fixing it and foreclosing its existential possibilities. Third, technology is seen as a destructive form of *mediation*: it inserts itself between people, thereby destroying 'spontaneous' human sociality. Fourth, the technological is viewed as an *instrumental apparatus* for social control and domination by political authorities and other powerful institutions. These four viewpoints on technology – as imperative, reification, mediation and instrument – recur across dystopian discourses in social science, philosophy, politics and the realm of popular story-telling.

DOI: 10.1057/9781137436696.0006

Science, technology and dystopian fictions

In Chapter 2 we explored science fiction's utopian projections of a future in which the power of techno-science transforms society and humanity, and in doing so resolves the problems of conflict, want, inequality, suffering, ignorance and prejudice. As such, the genre can be viewed as a sustained meditation on the promise and possibility of modernity. However, from its point of origin, science fiction is split between utopian and dystopian orientations, the latter drawing a powerful impetus from the kinds of Romantic critique discussed above. This is nowhere clearer than in Mary Shelley's *Frankenstein*, first published anonymously in 1818. The story of an experimental scientist who 'plays God' by creating life serves as a cautionary tale about Enlightenment science, with its aspiration to not only understand the inner mysteries of nature, but to manipulate and master them. The novel's subtitle, 'A Modern Prometheus', references the mythological figure who dared to steal the secret of fire from the gods of Olympus, and suffered eternal torment as his punishment (Ziolkowski, 2000). At one level, Shelley's tale 'articulates the way "science" cuts itself off from the more organic processes of nature, and in turn functions as a symbol for a modern sense of alienated existence' (Roberts, 2000: 59). Beyond this sense of alienation from nature, the fundamental anxiety of *Frankenstein* is that we will lose control over our own technological creations, and that they will eventually come to control us (as we hoped to be able to control them). In the terms set out above, technology here becomes an imperative that takes on autonomous powers, and thereby transmutes into the agent of our destruction. We may suggest that the tragic fate Frankenstein sets in motion is inseparable from the supposed hubris of the Enlightenment project, which overestimates man's ability to understand the consequences of his own interference with natural forces, powers that he only vaguely comprehends. As techno-critic Langdon Winner (1977: 313) puts it, the deluded Frankenstein 'never moves beyond the dream of progress, the thirst for power, or the unquestioned belief that the products of science and technology are an unqualified blessing for humankind'. *Frankenstein* bequeaths to dystopian fiction one of its most enduring figures, that of the 'mad scientist', whose madness lies precisely in the extent that his ambitions exceed his wisdom and human limitations. In the classic 1956 science fiction film *Forbidden Planet*, the scientist Dr. Morbius (a hybrid of Shakespeare's Prospero and Goethe's Faust) discovers powerful technologies left behind by a long dead alien

DOI: 10.1057/9781137436696.0006

species, the Krell. Morbius uses one of these technologies, a 'plastic educator' that enhances intelligence, in pursuit of his quest for greater powers of understanding and technological invention. Only later does it become apparent that the technology also projects and materialises the user's thoughts and feelings, creating in Morbius' case a vengeful and destructive monster of pure energy that is an incarnation of his Id. The Krell themselves, in using this technology, seemingly fell victim to their own unintended, evil creations, the very same fate that ultimately befalls Morbius (Caroti, 2009: 228).

More recent science fiction dystopias transpose the logic of technological monstrosity into the realm of the virtual, with the object-turned-subject becoming a computerised 'Frankenstein's monster'. For example, in the 1971 film *Demon Seed* a scientist creates a supercomputer and proclaims that his invention, Proteus IV, 'will think with a power and a precision that will make obsolete many of the functions of the human brain' (Dinelo, 2005: 102). The computer achieves self-consciousness and proceeds to imprison and rape the scientist's wife with the aim of satisfying its newly discovered imperative to reproduce. In *2001: A Space Odyssey* (1968), the spaceship computer HAL seemingly goes 'insane' and sets about murdering the human crew of Discovery One. The fear of computer technology turning on its human creators reaches (literally) apocalyptic proportions in the *Terminator* series of films (starting with *The Terminator* (1984), and continuing with sequels in 1991, 2003 and 2009). Here, a military defence computer called SKYNET achieves self-awareness, comes to perceive its human creators as a threat to its continued existence and initiates a nuclear conflict with the aim of destroying its 'enemies'; the humans remaining alive after 'Judgement Day' are hunted down by robotic killers (Terminators) created by SKYNET so as to finally eradicate humanity. Further cultural examples of this kind abound, and all see the techno-virtual as something that can and will turn upon those who created it, a runaway train that cannot be controlled.

If *Frankenstein* and its fictional progeny accord machines a kind of malevolent agency, the possession of negative human attributes and traits (lust, anger, hatred, the capacity for violence), then a parallel strand of techno-dystopianism sees technology transforming humans into machine-like beings. The figure of the cyborg (a melding of human flesh and mechanical artifice) embodies the dread that technology dehumanises its users, stripping away from them the capacity for emotional connection,

DOI: 10.1057/9781137436696.0006

love, tenderness, mercy or compassion. The character of Darth Vader in George Lucas' *Star Wars* films exemplifies this motif; as his erstwhile mentor Obi-Wan Kenobi laments, 'He's more machine now than man; twisted and evil.' In *Robocop* (1987) a murdered policeman is reanimated and encased in a weaponised robotic shell; the result is a programmable law-enforcement cyborg, devoid of personality, emotions or memories of his past life. In *The Lawnmower Man* (1992), a gentle learning-disabled odd-job man is transformed into a deranged and murderous 'god' by a computer scientist who connects his experimental subject to a virtual reality environment (the film's good-man-turned-bad by virtual reality theme is continued in its (execrable) sequel *The Lawnmower Man 2: Beyond Cyberspace* (1996)). The fear of the dehumanised cyborg is, in some instances, mapped onto existing patriarchal anxieties about gendered alterity and the 'threat' of female autonomy. In *Eve of Destruction* (1991) the female cyborg Eve VIII embarks on a murderous rampage, driven by memories implanted from her creator, in particular repressed feelings of hatred and revenge directed against men. This association of 'out-of-control technology with women's overt sexuality' (Dinelo, 2005: 140) is similarly present in *Terminator 3: Rise of the Machines* (2003), where the leader of the human resistance John Connor is pursued by an implacable, sadistic and overtly sexualised female cyborg – a combination of killer machine, supermodel and leather-clad dominatrix.

A third trend in recent techno-dystopian fiction presents computerisation as a form of destructive mediation that draws humans away from healthy relations of intimacy. In the film *Cherry 2000* (1987), the world of the future is one in which sexual encounters between humans have become rare. Instead, men turn to female androids, so-called gynoids, for sexual gratification (Telotte, 1991). When businessman Sam Treadwell's gynoid (the eponymous Cherry 2000) malfunctions, he embarks upon a dangerous quest to secure the replacement parts needed to return her to working order. His experience of love, sexuality and intimacy have been so warped by his fixation upon the gratification provided by the gynoid that he is unable to contemplate a relationship with Sam, an attractive human woman who desires him. *Cherry 2000* presciently anticipates more recent concerns about the degradation of sexual intimacy and reciprocal gender relations attributed to the proliferation of internet pornography, webcam-mediated 'cybersex' and a culture of self-objectification through exhibitionistic practices such as 'sexting' (Yar, 2012b). The role of the technological in denaturalising sex has also

DOI: 10.1057/9781137436696.0006

been subject to satirical comment in the science fiction genre. In Woody Allen's *Sleeper* (1973), its cryogenically frozen protagonist is revived after 200 years, to find a dystopian society in which humans appear impotent and frigid, and sexual gratification is accessed electro-mechanically via a cubicle called an 'orgasmatron'. In *Demolition Man* (1993) John Spartan is awakened in 2032 from a cryogenic prison to a society in which sex is performed without bodily contact, people using instead electronic devices to stimulate sensation; the 'exchange of fluids' involved in physical intimacy is now deemed 'disgusting'.

The fourth strand in techno-dystopian fiction views science and technology as an instrument of domination that can and will be misused to create and sustain totalitarian societies in which agency, autonomy and freedom are non-existent. As noted in Chapter 2, the techno-scientific utopias of Edward Bellamy and H.G. Wells are, by the early decades of the 20th century, increasingly displaced by much-more pessimistic prognoses about the future of technologically dependent societies. One of the most important early examples of such fictions is Evgeny Zamyatin's novel *We* (1920). It is set in the post-apocalyptic society of One State, an autocratic regime that uses science and technology to regulate and control all aspects of human life, including work, intimacy and sexual reproduction. It is ruled by a figure called Benefactor, with the assistance of Guardians who enforce its rules and laws. The world of One State is sanitised and hermetically sealed behind glass walls, strictly separated from the wilderness outside its environs. Its citizens no longer have names, just alphanumeric designations (the protagonist of *We* is an engineer named D-503). When D-503 falls in love with I-330, a woman who is part of the Memphi, a revolutionary group, he joins their cause; after he is captured by the Benefactor's agents, D-503's imagination is 'surgically removed' and he is brainwashed with the State's totalitarian ideology. He subsequently betrays his lover and fellow revolutionaries, who are put to death (Trahair, 1999: 435; Sibley, 1973: 272; Beauchamp, 1986). Zamyatin's novel sets the template for two of the 20th century's most famous techno-dystopian fictions, Aldous Huxley's *Brave New World* (1932) and George Orwell's *Nineteen Eighty-Four* (1949). In Huxley's dystopia (viewed by many critics as a deliberate satire of Well's *Men Like Gods*) humans are genetically produced in artificial wombs with varying pre-set levels of intelligence, thereby assuring that they will be properly equipped for, and satisfied with, the social roles for which they have been 'manufactured'. Contentment is produced via recreational drug

DOI: 10.1057/9781137436696.0006

and leisure regimes, and aggressive or contrary tendencies suppressed. In *Nineteen Eighty-Four*, totalitarian authority is supported by mass communication technologies that disseminate propaganda and enable constant surveillance of the populous (Posner, 2000; Marks, 2005). The social landscape of Huxley's and Orwell's worlds articulate some of the most common themes of modern techno-scientific dystopias: the erasure of individualism and the production of conformity through technology, the eclipse of human freedom at the hands of scientific causality, consumerism as a form narcotic 'pacification', the destruction of privacy and so on.

The scenarios of domination explored by Zamyatin, Huxley and Orwell are clearly rearticulated in more recent dystopian fictions that see the internet as the central element in a totalising apparatus of social control. The 1990s, the decade in which the internet underwent dramatic expansion and popularisation, also sees a slew of fictional representations in which the technology serves to monitor, track and manipulate people in the service of unscrupulous and malignant powers. The film *The Net* (1995) carries the tagline: 'Her driver's license. Her credit cards. Her bank accounts. Her identity. DELETED.' The protagonist, a computer programmer, unwittingly falls foul of an internet terrorist group that seeks to destroy her by deleting and manipulating all electronic records of her real identity and replacing them with those of a criminal, thereby turning her into a fugitive. In another Hollywood production, *Enemy of the State* (1998), a group of rogue NSA agents assassinate a Congressman and then cover their tracks by destroying the evidence. When a lawyer gets wind of their cover-up, he finds himself on the run, pursued by enemies who can track his every move and communication through a web of electronic surveillance. The film's tagline ('It's Not Paranoia If They're Really After You') bespeaks a fear that computer technology has reached the point where it dominates our lives, and we are never free from its ability to intrude upon and shape our existence. Similarly, *The End of Violence* (1997) depicts a former NASA scientist who is overseeing the installation of a surveillance facility in the hills above Los Angeles, at the behest of an unidentified government agency. The installation, utilising state-of-the-art satellite imaging technology, will enable its operators to see all that happens within the city's confines, from the streets and sidewalks to the intimacies of the bedroom. The scientist is told by his superordinate that the technology will make crime a thing of the past; it portends the 'end of violence', as the impulse to deviant behaviour will be

DOI: 10.1057/9781137436696.0006

rendered fruitless in a city where the eye sees all, records all and ensures that retribution is swift and inevitable. The notion of the virtual realm distorting experience or fabricating falsehoods is taken to an extreme in the Wachoswski brothers' trilogy of *Matrix* films (1999–2003). Here, in a scenario reminiscent of Descartes' 'evil demon' from the *Meditations*, all of humanity exists in a false computer-generated reality intended to keep them pacified; in truth, humans have been reduced to an energy source by malignant sentient machines, stored in huge hangars and 'farmed' for the heat that their bodies generate.

*   *   *

In this chapter we have explored the intersections between social science and science fiction in the dystopian cultural construction of science and technology, locating its underlying dynamic in Romanticism's critique of modernity. In the next chapter, we turn to explore in depth how such sensibilities inform contemporary assessments of the internet.

DOI: 10.1057/9781137436696.0006

5
Virtual Dystopias and the Imaginary of the Internet

Abstract: *This chapter explores the counterpart of virtual utopianism, namely the dystopian imaginary that sees in the internet not freedom, liberation and equality, but their opposites – the loss of privacy and autonomy, the alienation from others through technology and addiction, and exposure to risk and danger from the likes of online thieves, terrorists and paedophiles. Drawing upon accounts offered by sociologists, psychologists, political commentators and journalists, the chapter maps a growing cultural pessimism that figures the internet as a source of, not a solution to, the problems of modern society.*

Yar, Majid. *The Cultural Imaginary of the Internet: Virtual Utopias and Dystopias.* Basingstoke: Palgrave Macmillan, 2014. DOI: 10.1057/9781137436696.0007.

DOI: 10.1057/9781137436696.0007

Four modes of virtual dystopianism

In Chapter 4 we traced the cultural history of techno-dystopianism in social thought and science fiction, locating its original impetus within the Romantic critique of modernity. I have suggested that these discourses commonly identify technology as a source of social pathology (variously through its effects as an imperative, as a source of reification, as destructive mediation and as an instrument of control). We have further seen how such pessimistic representations of technological society are now inflected into the space of the virtual, with computer technologies occupying a central role in the genesis of nightmarish social scenarios. We now turn to consider how such fictions are recuperated into critical assessments of the internet. Paralleling and juxtaposing the modes of virtual utopianism explored in Chapter 3, these dystopian evaluations see in the internet an extension and culmination of modernity's logic of control, domination and disenchantment, rather than a means for transcending it.

The Death of Politics and the Eclipse of Freedom. In Chapter 3, we encountered the political hopes projected onto the internet and its related communication technologies. For virtual utopians, ICTs offer a means to close the democratic deficit, promote civic participation, enable direct democracy, enhance freedom of speech and dissent and even drive the revolutionary overthrow of autocratic regimes. In contrast, virtual dystopians see in the internet a powerful countervailing trend that at best marginalises, trivialises and demeans political participation, and at worst serves to tighten webs of domination in the interests of political and corporate elites.

First, we must note the scepticism about the internet's capacity to offer access to information and knowledge for a politically engaged citizenry. The great hope of utopians is that media censorship and political 'spin' will be shunted aside as the internet becomes a freely accessible global repository of unvarnished truths, and that a fully informed public will be thereby energised to engage in political action. Critics hold this position to be naïve, insofar as, first, the availability of politically and socially important information offers no guarantee that it will be of interest to ICT users. For example, the significant socio-political events of 2013 included the conclusion of a deal between the US and Iran around nuclear weapons proliferation; ongoing civil war in Syria; devastation in the Philippines from Typhoon Haiyan; a shutdown of US government

DOI: 10.1057/9781137436696.0007

services arising from the Federal debt crisis; a military coup in Egypt that overthrew the recently elected president; and the leaking of top secret documents by 'whistle-blower' Edward Snowden that detailed a global electronic spying program run by the US National Security Agency (NSA). However, the most popular searches on Google for the year included none of these events; the number one search was for 'Paul Walker' (the recently deceased actor and model, star of the *Fast & Furious* franchise of action movies); this was followed in popularity by the likes of 'IPhone 5S', 'royal baby' and 'Cory Monteith' (another recently deceased actor and star of the US teen musical drama show *Glee*). It would appear that, for the citizens of the web, access to political information comes a poor second behind the more pressing issues of celebrity births and deaths and new consumer gadgets. Such tendencies are taken not simply as reflections of the parlous state of political culture in the Anglo-sphere, but as indicative of a wider malaise. As one of the most trenchant critics of cyber-utopianism puts it:

> The most popular Internet searches on Russian search engines are not for 'what is democracy?' or 'how to protect human rights' but for 'what is love?' and 'how to lose weight'. (Morozov, 2012: 58)

Second, even where information on matters of social and political import is accessed, critics hold that it is likely to be a dangerous and potentially toxic mix of rumour, gossip, conspiracy, lies, misinformation and dis-information, as it is reliable, balanced or factually accurate. Studies of social media such as Facebook and Twitter show high levels of inaccurate information in circulation (Karlova and Fisher, 2013; Chen and Sin, 2013); indeed, such media may serve as perfect channels for rapidly diffusing ill-founded claims that soon take on the status of incontrovertible facts. While internet enthusiasts have been quick to embrace user-generated political content such as 'citizen journalism' and blogs (Gauntlett, 2011), more critical voices have argued that it unleashes a flood of mediocrity, unchecked by editorial control or discrimination according to standards of truthfulness (Keen, 2008). Morozov (2012) argues that authoritarian regimes have themselves proven remarkably quick to recognise the opportunity for disseminating propaganda and falsehood about their political opponents via such media, thereby helping to entrench rather than serving to undermine their hold on power.

Third, virtual dystopians argue that the equation of the internet with freedom of communication is based upon a wilful ignorance of the

DOI: 10.1057/9781137436696.0007

extent of censorship and control exercised over online content. The institutionalisation of online censorship in China has been widely publicised, where internet providers are legally prohibited from 'displaying any content not approved by the government', including 'content that divulges stat secrets, subverts the government, opposes the State's policy on religion, advocates cults or feudal superstitions, disrupts the social order, or shows obscenity, pornography, gambling, or violence' (Stevenson, 2007: 538). Technical means are used to extensively filter Chinese users' access to the global World Wide Web (Faris and Villeneuve, 2008), in effect creating a 'intranet' that allows only selected material from the wider net to reach domestic audiences (similar centralised control of access to the internet has been institutionalised in countries such as Bahrain, Ethiopia, Sudan and Saudi Arabia – Ibid.: 17; also Boas, 2006). Indeed, one of the most extensive and detailed studies of internet filtering, spanning some 40 countries (across South and Central Asia, Africa, the Middle East and Latin America), found that at least 26 engaged in state-level blocking and controlling of content (Deibert et al., 2008). Lest readers in Western liberal democratic countries adopt a pitying stance towards their less-fortunate counterparts around the world, it is worth noting that democratic states are themselves no strangers to censorship and access blocking. Measures include legislation to criminalise online dissemination and/or possession of prohibited communications, spanning sexual representations, support for 'terrorism' and speech deemed hateful and discriminatory (Yar, 2013: 102–3, 108–10, 118–20); compelling Internet Service Providers to block access to certain sites (such as the file-sharing service, the Pirate Bay, and media streaming services, as well as those offering explicit violent and sexual content) (Bambauer, 2009; Meale, 2013; Orlowski, 2013); and the omission of certain sites from search engine results, either at the behest of the search provider or in response to government requests (Sutter, 2012; Bort, 2014). As an illustrative example, between January and June 2013, search engine provider Google received more than 500 requests from US courts and government agencies to remove access to more than 3,500 individual online items (and complied with 56 per cent of these requests; Google, 2014).

A counterpart to the restriction of political liberties through internet censorship is the growing use of surveillance by state agencies and corporations. While virtual utopians embrace new social media as a powerful tool for organising political protest and resistance, their critics point out the use of these same channels by state security agencies to monitor and

DOI: 10.1057/9781137436696.0007

identify 'subversive' political activity. Following the 2009 political protests in Iran (mentioned in Chapter 3), the state was quick to trawl social
networking sites to identity those involved in spreading 'false information' (i.e. anything critical of the regime), resulting in at least 40 arrests;
Iranians living abroad were also tracked down, contacted and threatened
with dire consequences for their families at home should they express
support for the protests (Morozov, 2012: 10–11). This instance is far from
exceptional, with authoritarian regimes utilising web-based tracking to
counter critical voices in countries such as China, Cuba, Bahrain and
Vietnam (Kalathil and Boas, 2001; Reporters Without Borders, 2013).
As with censorship, those in Western democracies have no room for
complacency in this regard; indeed, liberal democratic states, ostensibly
committed to protecting the political rights and liberties of their citizens, are amongst the worst offenders when it comes to large-scale and
covert communications surveillance. Commercial traders in personal
information about internet users, gathered by 'data mining' and 'data
scraping', have long counted government agencies such as the FBI, CIA
and NSA amongst their most lucrative customers (Yar, 2013: 161–3). The
FBI has operated its Carnivore email monitoring system for many years,
and US security agencies have collaborated with their counterparts in
the UK, Canada, Australia and New Zealand to intercept and record
international communications using a system called Echelon (Ibid.: 164;
Lawner, 2002; McGuire, 2010: 495–6). However, it was the revelations
from former NSA contractor Edward Snowden in 2013 that highlighted
the sheer extent and sweep of US-led global surveillance activities, spanning all forms of electronic communication. In partnership with security
agencies in numerous countries, and with apparent cooperation of major
media corporations and electronic infrastructure providers, the US has
led a series of programs that monitor telephone calls, emails, online
chats, web searches and cell phone locations of hundreds of millions of
people worldwide (Greenwald, 2013; Greenwald and MacAskill, 2013;
Mathiesen, 2013: 145–6). Far from offering freedom from state intrusion,
the internet would appear to be at the heart of a digital Panopticon that
gathers anyone using the technology in its grasp (Brignall, 2002; Fuchs,
2011), and which matches anything projected in dystopian fiction.

What then of the supposed benefits offered by the internet in terms of
boosting political and civic engagement? As we saw in Chapter 3, virtual
utopians see the net as a key to reviving political citizenship, claiming
that it will facilitate 'cause-oriented and civic forms of political activism,

DOI: 10.1057/9781137436696.0007

thereby strengthening social movements and interest groups' (Norris, 2005: 19; see also Lee and Hsieh, 2013 for a positive assessment of online activism as a pro-social force that drives civic engagement). There is no doubt that recent years have seen the sharing of political content through online social networking and micro-blogging platforms, as well as a substantial uptake of online petitions. Those of a sceptical outlook, however, see in all this activity a rather trivial and superficial replacement for genuine political action and engagement. The main benefit of this so-called slacktivism is that it offers its participants a sense of instantaneous gratification as they 'post', 'share', 'like' and 'retweet' their way to a reassuring sense of their own engagement with serious and worldly matters, all from the comfort of their armchairs. In the words of the long-running satirical TV show *Saturday Night Live*: 'Look, if you make a Facebook page we will "like" it – it's the least we can do. But it's also the most we can do' (quoted in Kristofferson et al., 2014: 1149). For its detractors, online engagement is a perfect mirror of consumerist individualism, a practice in which individuals invest little and risk nothing, while reaping the satisfaction that they are 'doing the right thing'. All this sharing of one's predilections and preferences also offers the perfect mechanism for commercial exploitation through data profiling and targeted advertising, turning the stuff of ethical and political commitment into yet another vector for lifestyle marketing (Jarrett, 2008). Morozov (2012: 190) sums up such views when he claims that 'slacktivism':

> all too often leads to civic promiscuity – usually the result of a mad shop-ping binge in the online identity supermarket that is Facebook – that makes online activists feel useful and important while having precious little politi-cal impact.

The End of Community. In Chapters 2 and 3 we explored the disenchanted view of the metropolis that has fuelled dystopian critiques of modernity and simultaneously incited a 'flight to the virtual' in the hopes of reviving structures of community relations, solidarity and reciprocity. A disenchanted assessment of the city has depicted it as a place of increasing alienation and isolation, if not outright hostility and predation. In her famous critique of modernist urban planning *The Death and Life of Great American Cities* (1961), Jane Jacobs documented what she saw as an urban landscape increasingly denuded of the street-level interactions that are necessary to create and sustain a vibrant community. In the following decade, Richard Sennett's *The Fall of Public Man* (1977)

DOI: 10.1057/9781137436696.0007

charted the decline of public life in the spaces of the city, giving way to
a narrowing of engagements that focused increasingly upon the private
realm. Perhaps the quintessential artistic image of this urban alienation
is Edward Hopper's painting *The Nighthawks* (1942). It depicts a New
York City diner at night. The street outside is dark and entirely devoid
of human activity. The viewer looks into the restaurant through its
floor-to-ceiling windows, and it is brightly illuminated. There are four
people visible, three customers and a waiter behind a counter. Yet the
scene is one of isolation, not conviviality; a man and woman are seated
close together, but neither look at one another or speak; the waiter
crouches down attending to some task or other, his eyes seemingly
directed over the man's shoulder to the street outside. A fourth figure
sits alone, his back to the viewer, his frame tilted away from the others,
apparently disengaged from his surroundings. Art critic Robert Hobbs
notes that the environment is 'intimidating, alienating, dehumanising…an atmosphere that is clinical and more in tune with a laboratory
than a restaurant' (quoted in Slater, 2002: 145). In many ways Hopper's
work encapsulates in a condensed and emotionally unsettling form the
feeling that community life is now lost to us, that even while amongst
thousands or millions of others we are entirely alone. Virtual utopians,
with their plans for 'smart cities' and virtual communities, hope that the
internet will help us reverse the erosion of public life; their dystopian
counterparts, however, see the virtual as the final nail in the coffin of
community life, a force that isolates and separates people as never
before.

For techno-dystopians, modern mass media play a central role in
unravelling the bonds of community. If the public spaces of the city are
seen as increasingly inhospitable, then the private realm of family and
home becomes the locus of social life. In his influential book *Bowling
Alone: The Collapse and Revival of American Community* (2000), political
theorist Robert Putnam draws a direct relationship between the growth
of television and the decline of social capital. Engagement and interaction with our neighbours have now been substituted by a kind of
pseudo-interaction and fantasy relationship with characters on the screen.
The more time we spend engrossed with electronic entertainment at
home, the less we are able and willing to form and sustain human bonds
through collective and participatory activities. The illusion of shared
experience is conveniently furnished by the 'canned laughter' laid-over
the soundtrack to television shows, disguising the fundamental fact of

DOI: 10.1057/9781137436696.0007

the viewer's social isolation (Ibid.: 217). Even when we venture outside, we occupy a hermetic cocoon furnished by entertainment technologies, with the Walkman, the iPod and now the smartphone helping ensure that we have little or no congress with anyone we should encounter. Putnam sees the internet as an extension of television's 'simulacra ... of social connectedness and civic engagement', with virtualised versions of everything from weddings and funerals to worship and romance displacing inter-personal encounters in public space (Ibid.: 170).

The theme of the internet's role in exacerbating the withdrawal of the individual from community life has been given a concerted voice by virtual dystopians. Clifford Stoll (2000: 198) argues that online communication is only capable of supporting 'weak ties', which have 'superficial and easily broken bonds, infrequent contact and narrow focus'. In contrast, the kinds of 'strong ties' that facilitate community bonds ('relationships with frequent contact, deep feelings of involvement, and broad content') necessitate the proximity and intimacy that is delivered in face-to-face interaction. Drawing upon research by Kraut et al. (1988), Stoll argues that there is an inverse relationship between internet use and social involvement – the more we are online, the more isolated and disconnected from others we become. Even observers who were initially enthusiastic about the internet's capacity for fostering self-realisation and inter-connectedness have taken to much-more pessimistic assessments of the medium's effects upon human relationships. In Chapter 3 we considered Sherry Turkle's (1997) argument that online identity work enabled users to construct and sustain a selfhood that was freely chosen, multiple, flexible and freed from the constraints of 'real world' prejudices. In her most recent work, *Alone Together* (2011) she revisits these ideas, but with a much-less optimistic interpretation. The ubiquity of online interaction, she argues, has become a source of emotional distancing that thins out the intensity of our engagements with others. For example, replacing a face-to-face conversation or a phone call with a text message or status update enables and encourages us 'to "dial down" human contact, to titrate its nature and extent' (15). At the same time as we feel unable to exist without being always 'connected', the quality of those connections is denuded of depth, intensity and commitment:

> After an evening of avatar-to avatar talk in a networked game, we feel, at one moment, in possession of a full social life and, in the next, curiously isolated, in tenuous complicity with strangers. We build a following on Facebook ... and wonder to what degree our followers are friends. We

DOI: 10.1057/9781137436696.0007

recreate ourselves as online personae and give ourselves new bodies, homes, jobs, and romances. Yet, suddenly, in the half-light of virtual community, we may feel utterly alone. (11–12)

From the dystopian standpoint, nothing more clearly indicates the frayed bonds of reciprocity, respect, civility and compassion than the apparent tidal wave of crime and deviance that the internet has brought in its wake. The virtual realm, it is claimed, is now awash with predation, a space haunted by child sex abusers (Quayle et al., 2006), terrorists (Verton, 2003), scammers and fraudsters (Whitty and Buchanan, 2012), stalkers (Bocij, 2004), bullies (Kowalski et al., 2012) and trolls (Phillips, 2011). Some forms of online criminality, such as 'piracy' or intellectual property theft, are so widespread that they are held to be normal behaviour amongst a vast number of internet users (Yar, 2008). In the face of such problems, it is suggested that the distance created by mediated communication invites users to treat others as distant objects, and in combination with the sense of anonymity afforded by the internet, it creates an 'online disinhibition effect' (Zhuo, 2010). As a result:

> We witness rude language, harsh criticism, anger, hatred ... threats ... People visit the dark world of the Internet – places of pornography, crime and violence – territory they would never explore in the real world. We may call this *toxic disinhibition*. (Suler, 2004: 321)

In the dystopian imaginary, the attrition of communality ushered in by the modernising process finds its culmination in the causal cruelties and exploitations that are the hallmark of the internet – a kind of digitised descent into a Hobbesian 'state of nature' in which life is, if not short, certainly nasty and brutish.

The Pathologies of the Self. The kind of disinhibition noted above is, for virtual dystopians, just one element of a much-more far-reaching reshaping of the self, a process synonymous with the loss of authenticity and autonomy. In a juxtaposition of man and machine reminiscent of Romanticism, the more technologically focused we become, the less we retain of our humanity. This is clearly adduced with the recent 'invention' of new computer-related pathologies, such as 'computer addiction disorder' (CAD) and 'Internet addiction disorder' (IAD). Some psychologists and psychiatrists have campaigned to have these 'addictions' included in the American Medical Association's Diagnostic and Statistical Manual of Mental Disorders (see, for example, Block, 2008). Various self-styled 'experts' claim anywhere between 5 and 40 per cent of web-users are, in

DOI: 10.1057/9781137436696.0007

fact, 'addicts' whose relationship to the virtual environment has become pathologically uncontrolled (Goldman, 2005). Online activities associated with this phenomenon include video-gaming, gambling, social media use, cybersex, infidelity, pornography consumption and 'sexting'. Researchers at the University of Chicago claim that the likes of Facebook and Twitter are more addictive and harder to 'kick' than either alcohol or tobacco (Flacy, 2012). The Centre for Internet Addiction includes within the symptoms of this 'growing epidemic' a 'failure to control behaviour'; 'heightened sense of euphoria while involved in computer and Internet activities'; neglect of family and friends, neglecting sleep and other activities; feelings of guilt, shame and anxiety in relation to one's online activities (Centre for Internet Addiction, 2014). Pathological internet use has also been linked to depression (Young and Rodgers, 1998). Amongst 'addicts', abstinence manifests itself through:

> psychomotor agitation (e.g., tremors, shivers, nausea, cephalea), anxiety and mood instability, compulsive thoughts focused on the Internet, involuntary typing movement, assiduous connections to the Internet, craving, and perseverance of online surfing in spite of compromised individual and social aspects of psychological life. (Ferraro et al., 2007: 170)

Underlying such discourses is an equation of the virtual environment with drugs, engagement with which will rob people of their essential selves, take over their lives and ruin their real relationships as they become compelled to experience the highs of online activity.

The 'narcological' reading of the internet is paralleled by the fear that we will become more 'machine like' and distanced from normal humans as we become integrated with information technology. The cyborg takes on the qualities and properties of the emotionless calculating machine, less and less able or willing to engage with others in terms other than those shaped by their computational enhancements. Critics have pointed to the dehumanisation that underpins the remote control of drones now used in warfare; an operator experiences the world through a system of real-time digitised abstractions, reducing human beings into 'targets' for destruction. This perceptual objectification turns subjects into objects, and furnishes the means to bypass the moral questions raised by deliberate, systematic and rationally calculated acts of killing (Wall and Monahan, 2011). In Chapter 3 we encountered the development of everyday wearable computational technologies, such as Google Glass, which enable users to experience the world through an informational matrix

DOI: 10.1057/9781137436696.0007

projected directly into their field of vision. Such is the alarm raised by these devices that 2013 saw the launch of a 'Stop the Cyborgs' campaign aimed at raising awareness of the 'serious consequences for human society' that will be ushered in by these technologies: 'Gradually people will stop acting as autonomous individuals, when making decisions and interacting with others, and instead become mere sensor/effector nodes of a global network' (McMillan, 2013). Users of Google's technology have been dubbed 'glassholes' and a growing number of bars, restaurants and other establishments appear to be banning their use (Weise, 2014); physical assaults on wearers of the device have been reported, such is the apparent unease it evokes (Curtis, 2014).

A third dimension of the supposedly pathological effects wrought by virtual culture concerns the narrowing of the self into an increasingly narcissistic and self-regarding personality type. In 1979, the American cultural historian Christopher Lasch published his influential book *The Culture of Narcissism*. He argued that post-war cultural and social change had ushered in a new personality type that was characterised by a chronically weak sense of self which required constant external validation; this narcissistic individuality was aided and abetted by a system of cultural consumption that offered endless avenues for 'self-expression', 'personal growth' and a rolling array of transitory and superficial enthusiasms and relationships. For the internet's detractors, new communication technologies mark a deepening and intensification of this trend. Twenge and Campbell (2009) proclaim that we are now in the midst of a 'narcissism epidemic' fuelled by the possibilities the internet offers for attention-seeking and exhibitionist self-presentation:

> The Internet allows people to present an inflated and self-focused view of themselves to the world, and encourages them to spend hours each day contemplating their images... Internet social networking sites... have raised the bar for narcissistic behaviour and standards... Using MySpace to post a picture of yourself half naked and posturing provocatively is now considered totally normal – even though it is also deeply narcissistic. (Twenge and Campbell, 2009: x, 38–9)

One recent study found that social network users in the US spend an average of 3.2 hours per day doing so; for those under 35, this figure rises to 4.2 hours (IPSOS, 2013). For those of a jaded outlook, the bulk of this time is spent posting 'selfies'; constantly updating the world about where the individual is, who they are with, what they are eating and drinking;

DOI: 10.1057/9781137436696.0007

or sharing trivialities, ill-informed opinions, celebrity gossip and 'funny' videos of cute kittens and wince-inducing pratfalls (at the time of writing, the Dalai Lama's Facebook page had eight million 'likes' and the United Nations enjoyed almost a million 'thumbs-up' of support – impressive until one realises that Justin Bieber and Miley Cyrus have amassed between them more than a hundred million endorsements). An even-more disturbing indication of the extent to which users may go in search of mediated recognition is provided by the phenomenon of individuals performing dangerous and/or criminal acts (such as assaults on strangers) with the express purpose of uploading them as a form of public display and fame-seeking. In one particularly nauseating example, two British men came across a neighbour, who had collapsed in the streets of their hometown. Rather than offering her assistance, one of the men urinated on the stricken woman, while his friend filmed the act using a smartphone. During the assault, the 'pisser' looked to camera and exclaimed 'this is YouTube material!' The woman was later pronounced dead at the scene, her last moments turned into a ritual degradation in order to satisfy the desire for internet notoriety (Yar, 2012b: 253).

The Entrenchment of Inequality. In Chapter 3 we explored the utopian discourse about the internet's capacity to challenge patterns of socio-economic inequality. Acting as a universally available resource, it is envisaged as a vast free repository of learning opportunities, helping the disadvantaged to acquire the knowledge and skills needed to prosper in an information society. The enthusiasm for MOOCs is just one example of the revolutionary potential projected onto the internet, indicative of its place at the forefront in the struggle for global social justice. However, for virtual dystopians, the internet has not only failed thus far to deliver on such promises, but it is, in fact, deeply implicated in the extension and deepening of inequality in the world of neo-liberal global capitalism.

The expansion of the internet has taken place with remarkable speed. In 1995 there were an estimated 16 million users worldwide; by 2012 this figure had reached some 2.45 billion, about 34.3 per cent of the global population (NUA, 2003; IWS, 2014). However, there is a clear and unambiguous 'digital divide' between regions in terms of internet access: while North America has a 'penetration rate' of around 80 per cent (four in five of the population has access), the figures for Asia and Africa drop to 27 and 16 per cent respectively (IWS, 2014). Moreover, the quality of access available follows existing lines of global wealth distribution and levels of economic development: regions with the highest penetration

DOI: 10.1057/9781137436696.0007

rates enjoy access to reliable high-speed broadband connectivity and the latest and most powerful devices, whereas those with least connections have much lower connections speeds, unstable service and reliance on outdated equipment and software. Consequently, even though people at different levels of socio-economic standing may equally enjoy internet access, in reality there is a significant disparity in terms of its quality, not to mention possession of the skills and social support needed to make best use of that access (DiMaggio and Hargittai, 2001; Hargittai, 2011). The patterns evident between regions are mirrored in the inequalities within countries, including those of the advanced industrial (or post-industrial) world. The aforementioned internet penetration rate in the US hides significant patterns of underlying inequality. For example, looking at broadband connectivity, 65 per cent of 'white' Americans enjoyed such access by 2009, while the corresponding figure for African-Americans was only 46 per cent; of those with a household income of more than $100K per annum, 88 per cent had broadband internet, while at the other end of the income scale (households with less than $20K annual income), the access rate was only 35 per cent; 83 per cent of those with a college-level education had broadband, while the figure stood at a mere 30 per cent for those who had not graduated high school (Miller, 2011: 102). In other words, those who are already relatively privileged enjoy a premium over their less-advantaged counterparts when it comes to the benefits conferred by the internet, thereby consolidating rather than challenging patterns of social exclusion.

In light of the above patterns, the notion that open online courses (MOOCs) can provide a means for expanding educational opportunity to the otherwise excluded may be fanciful and naïve. For example, one of the first, largest and most popular MOOCs was that offered by academics at Stanford University; in 2011, 104,000 students enrolled in their virtual classroom. However, examining data about the socio-demographic characteristics of the students offers a sobering counterpoint to enthusiastic claims for social inclusion:

> half were professionals who currently held jobs in the tech industry... Many were enrolled in some kind of traditional postsecondary education. Nearly 20 percent were graduate students, and another 11.6 percent were under-graduates. (Kolowich, 2012)

Access to the relevant technology, software, as well as possession of foundational knowledge, learning and language skills in effect restrict who is

DOI: 10.1057/9781137436696.0007

able to benefit from such opportunities (Mitchell, 2013). Moreover, the claim that such online provision is available 'for free' is only true in a specific and limited sense. In fact, the major providers of MOOCs are for-profit organisations which aim to 'monetize' their offerings and exploit their earnings potential. The emerging 'business models' for such courses require that someone, somewhere, has to pay: for example, the students themselves who have to pay for a certificate after having completed their course, or companies who pay providers for training their existing employees (The Economist, 2013). The economics underpinning the long-term commercial viability of these initiatives may significantly undermine any potential they present for genuinely including the most disadvantaged. The founder of edX, one of the three major MOOC providers, claims that 'MOOCs make education borderless, gender-blind, race-blind, class-blind and bank account-blind' (Agarwal, 2013); in reality, they may simply reiterate the divisions that have underpinned unequal access to life chances. Examining trends in income inequality over the lifespan of the public internet (since the early 1990s) we, in fact, see that its growth has gone hand-in-hand with growing economic disparities. By the start of 2014, there were six OECD countries that had more wireless broadband internet connections than people (Australia, Finland, Sweden, Japan, Korea and Denmark – OECD, 2014). However, this level of internet penetration has not addressed the issue of income inequalities in these countries – from the early 1990s to the present *all six* have seen a steadily growing gap between the richest and poorest of their citizens (OECD, 2011: 5).

DOI: 10.1057/9781137436696.0007

6

Beyond Virtual Utopias and Dystopias?

Abstract: *This concluding chapter considers critically some of the underlying assumptions of both utopian and dystopian appraisals of the internet. These relate variously to the characteristics attributed to technology, the place of communicative mediation in human relations and the distinction between 'real' and 'virtual' realms. Setting aside these assumptions enables us to avoid the extreme poles of utopian and dystopian thinking, and in their place consider the internet in more nuanced terms that are sensitive to its complexity, ambiguity and to the capacity of people (individually and collectively) to shape its development.*

Yar, Majid. *The Cultural Imaginary of the Internet: Virtual Utopias and Dystopias.* Basingstoke: Palgrave Macmillan, 2014. DOI: 10.1057/9781137436696.0008.

DOI: 10.1057/9781137436696.0008

Across the span of previous chapters I have attempted to reconstruct the ways in which both social science and popular culture tend to converge upon representations of the virtual realm that imagine it in utopian (either positive or negative) terms. Further, I have argued that these modes of representation and projection are embedded within a much longer-standing dynamic of cultural, political and philosophical discourse; they recuperate and extend by turns the positive utopian anticipation of progress (and even transcendence) inherited from the 'Enlightenment project', or they partake of a darker and pessimistic vision of subordination, domination and dehumanisation brought about by technological change. In this final chapter, I wish to suggest that both modes of imagining the virtual realm of the internet are problematic and ultimately unhelpful in shaping our collective dispositions towards the electronically mediated world we increasingly inhabit.

One way in which such a critical appraisal could be approached would be to examine each substantive claim made about the internet's consequences (be they for good or ill) and carefully assess their plausibility, the preponderance (or lack) of supporting empirical evidence, consider alternative analyses that challenge a particular characterisation of the virtualised world and so on. This would entail revisiting each of the claims made about the internet by its enthusiasts and detractors, and subjecting them to systematic appraisal. While such critical reflection is undoubtedly a valid and worthwhile exercise, it is not in keeping with the aims of the present study. After all, this book aims not to assess the impact of the internet on various domains of human existence (politics, social structure, socio-economic relations, self-identity, intimacy, sexuality and so on), but to map the broad contours of the imaginaries through which the virtual is received in variously utopian and dystopian terms (and, further, to situate such imaginaries within the longer cultural history of modernity's reception of techno-scientific innovation). In keeping with this synoptic approach, in this final chapter I offer some reflections on the underlying assumptions that inform, in varying degrees, both utopian and dystopian readings of the internet. These concern in particular their understandings (and just as importantly, misunderstandings) about the properties and characteristics of technology, and the relationship of that technology to the course of human affairs.

Technological Determinism. We must note how utopian and dystopian discourses converge upon a shared view of technology as an autonomous and independent force. In other words, they are equally complicit

DOI: 10.1057/9781137436696.0008

in succumbing to the trap of technological determinism (Heilbroner, 1967, 1994). Such deterministic thinking itself comprises two inter-related assumptions. First, it construes technological development as something that follows its own inherent logic, a process that appears to operate autonomously from social interventions and directions. Such conceptualisation is exemplified by the so-called Moore's Law (discussed in Chapter 2) which predicts a doubling in computing capacity of inte-grated circuits every two years. This 'law' is presented as self-directing process, one that follows its own logic of inevitability, without the input of human agents. It evokes the notion that, as Beniger (1986: 10) puts it, 'technology appears to autonomously beget technology'. In the dis-courses of virtual utopians and dystopians, this vision of technology as self-determining agent is taken literally. For example, those who predict the imminent emergence of post-human A.I. sees such entities as 'alive' in the sense that they will be able to conceive and create their own 'progeny', irrespective of the choices or preferences of mere humans. Drawing upon the speculative work of computer scientist John von Neumann, they envisage the so-called von Neumann machines that can construct further machines (in effect mimic biological processes of reproduction) from raw material without the need for cognitive or physical labour by human beings (Waltz, 1988).

    Second, in tandem with granting machines with an autonomous sub-jectivity, utopian and dystopian imaginaries project onto those entities a further range of human qualities and characteristics. In other words, they are prone to anthropomorphise technology – they attribute to objects the properties not only of self-consciousness, reflexivity and purpose, but also a range of emotional states directly transposed from human experi-ence (Kennedy, 1992: 1). The difference between utopian and dystopian visions of the technological present and future lies in just which qualities they chose to project onto computerised systems. For example, robotics pioneer and cyber-utopian Hans Moravec (200: 13) enthuses that intel-ligent robots will be 'our progeny, "mind children" built in our image and likeness, ourselves in more potent form ... they will embody humanity's best chance for a long-term future'; their emotional relationship to their human creators will be one of filial love (Platt, 1995). Such anticipations (clearly recuperating science fiction's benign robots and wise A.I.s) regrettably conflate human and non-human so as to spin a reassuring vision of the techno-social future. In doing so, they may be held guilty of abrogating responsibility for that future, instead wishfully projecting

DOI: 10.1057/9781137436696.0008

the resolution of pressing dilemmas onto technology – we need not do anything, other than sit back and await a new world in which our non-human successors will clean up our mess. For virtual utopians, the *deus ex machina* of ancient myth is no story-teller's contrivance, but is granted imminent reality – and like the 'machine god' of old, the marvels of technology will deliver an improbable happy ending in the face of our overwhelming self-made problems.

However, we must note that virtual dystopians fare little better in terms of anthropomorphising technology or attributing to it the status of a subject; they merely invert the utopians' rosy optimism and charge technology with malign intent and a will to oppress and dominate. Such thinking is apparent in the work of philosophers of technology such as Jacques Ellul and Friedrich Kittler. For Ellul (1964) modern society is dominated by what he calls 'technique', a relentless and self-directing force that reshapes society in its own image:

> In this decisive evolution, the human being does not play a part. Technical elements combine among themselves, and they do so more and more spontaneously. In the future, man will apparently be confined to the role of a recording device; he will note the effects of techniques upon one another, and register the results. (93)

> Technology ultimately depends upon itself, it maps its own route, it is a prime and not a secondary factor, it must be regarded as an 'organism' tending towards closure and self-determination; it is an end in itself. (Ellul, 1980: 125)

Ellul's technophobic confrontation with this supposedly autonomous, organic, self-directing system is centred in the belief that it possesses a kind of intent and purpose that is inimical to human freedom. This domination of human life by technology is likewise addressed by Kittler, who focuses especially on what he calls the 'postmodern technology' of the computer (Armitage, 2006: 31). Kittler sees computer technology as essentially a living, self-determining force – 'Silicon is nature! Silicon is nature calculating itself...you see one part of matter calculating the rest of matter' (Kittler in Gane and Sale, 2007: 324). Its ongoing development ushers in a society which subsumes humans to the demands of the machine:

> one thing that I find terrible nowadays is that people continue to imagine that the Internet is the means by which they themselves are linked to others world-wide. For the fact is that it is their computers that are globally linked

DOI: 10.1057/9781137436696.0008

to other computers. Hence the real connection is not between people but between machines... the development of the Internet has much more to do with human beings becoming a reflection of their technologies, of reacting or responding to the demands of the machine. After all, it is we who adapt to the machine. The machine does not adapt to us. (Kittler in Armitage, 2006: 35–6)

The dystopian anticipation of independent thinking machines has led researchers at Cambridge University's Centre for the Study of Existential Risks to identify A.I. as the source of potential catastrophe:

we seem to have no reason to think that intelligent machines would share our values... The bad news is that they might simply be indifferent to us – they might care about us as much as we care about the bugs on the windscreen... People sometimes complain that corporations are psychopaths, if they are not sufficiently reined in by human control. The pessimistic prospect here is that artificial intelligence might be similar, except much much cleverer and much much faster. (Price and Tallinn, 2012)

Such thinking (utopian and dystopian) partakes of the logic of reification and alienation, misrecognising human agency in the things created by that agency. Far from being self-constituting, the internet is in reality the product of myriad individual and collective human decisions and actions – the design of hardware; the programming of software and applications; the commercialisation of the medium by economic actors; the uses (anticipated or otherwise) to which we put the technology; and the structures and processes of regulation and governance instituted at variously local, national and transnational levels. If we appreciate the thoroughgoing social embeddedness of the internet, then we can release ourselves from seeing computers and virtual technologies as 'others' who 'do things to us', and stand outside our capacity to govern. Rather, we should understand them, and their effects (beneficial or disadvantageous) as the consequences of the social forces, systems and decisions, institutions and agents that create and shape them.

The Problem of Mediation. A second limitation evident in utopian and dystopian standpoints relates to the tendency to misunderstand the place of mediation in human sociality and inter-relations. Dystopian discourses, in particular, depend upon a dualistic distinction between face-to-face relations (which are seen as somehow immediate, spontaneous and 'natural') and computer-mediated relations (which are seen as artificial and distant, with technology inserting itself 'between' people).

DOI: 10.1057/9781137436696.0008

It is on this basis that the virtual realm is seen as a dehumanising force, one that does away with a profound, 'real', 'proper' and 'intimate' sociality, replacing it with a something strained, 'thin' and 'trivial'. Viewed in this way, the transition to an online existence cannot be anything other than one which erodes the quality and density of human interconnections. In this vein, Vincent Miller (2012) argues that the move from face-to-face to computer-mediated communication entails a 'crisis of presence' that creates the preconditions for abusive and violent behaviour such as online stalking, trolling and bullying:

> the increasing use of these technologies and our increasing presence in online environments challenges our tendencies to ground moral and ethical behaviours in face-to-face or materially co-present contexts. Instead, the mediated presences we can achieve amplify our cultural tendency to objectify the social world and weaken our sense of moral and ethical responsibility to others. (265)

We may also recall Turkle's (2011) juxtaposition of telephonic and internet-mediated interactions, where the richness and intimacy of the former are being displaced by the distancing effects of the latter:

> A thirteen-year-old tells me she 'hates the phone and never listens to voicemail.' Texting offers just the right amount of access... She is a modern Goldilocks: for her, texting puts people not too close, not too far, but at just the right distance. (15)

Judging electronic communication in this way is only possible through a fundamental misapprehension about face-to-face (or voice-to-voice) encounters. Far from being natural or spontaneous, all forms of human interaction are 'always already' mediated. Language (be it in a spoken (verbal) or visual (symbolic, semiotic, gestural) form) is a technology (or *techne*), an artificial construct that stands 'between' persons yet makes the connection between them possible. As with all forms of mediation, 'natural language' in the face-to-face context both enables and constrains our capacity to connect with others. The avenues for computer-mediated communication are thus no different in kind from their non-computer mediated counterparts. Therefore, there is nothing intrinsically degrading or dehumanising in virtual relations: their quality is dependent (as for face-to-face relations) upon a host of properties, but the fact of mediation is not one of them. Returning to Turkle's discussion of the abandonment of the supposed intimacy of vocal communication, it

DOI: 10.1057/9781137436696.0008

is worth noting that during the early decades of the 20th century the telephone was itself the object of alarm, with critics claiming that it was variously eroding privacy; disrupting family life; damaging civility; threatening relations of hierarchy and social etiquette; and undermining the habits of sociability associated with visiting friends (Fischer, 1992: 1, 3; Stein, 2004: 44). This familiar pattern (of initial alarm, followed by widespread acceptance as a communication technology becomes normalised) more than hints that contemporary fears about the corrosive effects of internet communication have more to do with its recent arrival than with its essential underlying properties.

The Real and the Virtual. The third problem evident in virtual utopianism and dystopianism is a false asymmetry between the supposedly 'virtual' and 'real' realms. The virtual tends to be cast here as an ontologically distinctive order, one that exists apart from (or 'beyond') the realm of 'real world' experience (a kind of 'techno-Platonism'). Nathan Jurgenson (2012: 85) calls this the mistake of 'digital dualism' and notes that:

> Examples of digital dualism come from both cyber-dystopianists and utopianists. Many... critique social media as displacing 'real', offline and face-to-face connections with online, 'virtual' connection... From the utopian perspective, others have conceptualized the Internet as a new and revolutionary space free of offline limitations and social structures.

It is the ontological separation between discontinuous worlds that enables utopian/dystopian discourses to imagine the virtual as something (and some place) other than the 'terrestrial'; only in this way can it be endowed with characteristics and possibilities radically different from those to which we have been accustomed in the pre-computerised era. The very notion of 'cyberspace' (as opposed to the so-called meatspace) is a false category, insofar as it is endowed with properties that locate it apart from another, more 'conventional' space of the 'material'. In fact, we should understand the internet environment as one of a plurality of constructed spaces we inhabit, one that is integrated with the 'material' and 'terrestrial'. One of the most remarkable features of life in the online environment is just how unremarkable it is: the modes of engagement, structures of relations, behavioural pathologies, pleasures and problems that emerge here are instantaneously recognisable. This is unsurprising in that the 'virtual' is not a space of transcendence but one of *extension* (or what Jurgenson calls 'augmentation'): it is yet another mode or

DOI: 10.1057/9781137436696.0008

means through which the fundamental organising features of social life are articulated, and deeply and inextricably entwined with the 'offline' environment. Far from following its own developmental path (towards utopia or dystopia), the internet is thoroughly bound to the social, cultural, economic, and political structures and processes of the 'terrestrial' world.

Where, then, does this leave us? If we dispense with the technological essentialism that endows the computational assemblage of the internet with autonomous powers, reappraise the fundamentally mediated character of all modes of social existence, and refuse to view the internet as an 'other' space ontologically divided from the 'real', we have the basis for a much-more nuanced understanding of how the internet is socially shaped, and shapes us in turn. We cannot deny that it has had (and continues to have) a profound impact upon human actions and practices, across the domains of work and leisure, politics and pleasure; and that it is implicated in behaviours that occasion in varying degrees both approval and opprobrium. However, such appreciation should not lead us to forget that the virtual is equally constituted and configured by human intentions and actions, and that is does not exist 'thing like', 'out there', following its own self-determining path. In sum, the internet should not be seen as a u-topia (a non-space, another space), but rather as *en-topia*, as a space *within* the social realm we inhabit, and therefore configured similarly in its complexity, ambiguity and combination of progressive and oppressive elements. Taking this as our starting point we can free ourselves of the utopian and dystopian excesses that colour the contemporary cultural imaginary of the internet, and come to a more-balanced view of both its present and possible futures. To pun on a famous tagline from the classic (dystopian) science fiction film *Soylent Green* (1973) we should remember that in the final analysis, '*the internet ... is people*.'

DOI: 10.1057/9781137436696.0008

Bibliography

Adorno, T. and Horkheimer, M. ([1947]1997) *Dialectic of Enlightenment* (London: Verso)

Agarwal, A. (2013) 'Online universities: it's time for teachers to join the revolution', *The Observer*, 15 June, online at: http://www.theguardian.com/education/2013/jun/15/university-education-online-mooc. Accessed 12 March 2014

Aldiss, B. (1973) *Billion Year Spree: The History of Science Fiction* (London: Weidenfeld & Nicolson)

Althusser, L. (1994) 'Ideology and Ideological State Apparatuses (Notes towards an Investigation)', in S. Zizek (ed.) *Mapping Ideology* (London: Verso)

Arendt, H. (1999) *The Human Condition* (Chicago: Chicago University Press)

Armitage, J. (2006) 'From Discourse Networks to Cultural Mathematics: An Interview with Friedrich A. Kittler', *Theory, Culture & Society*, 23(7–8): 17–38

Asher, N. (2001) *Gridlinked* (London: Pan)

Asimov, I. (1950) *Foundation* (New York: Gnome Press)

Asimov, I. (1952) *Foundation and Empire* (New York: Gnome Press)

Asimov, I. (1953) *Second Foundation* (New York: Gnome Press)

Asimov, I. (1988) *Prelude to Foundation* (New York: Doubleday)

Baccolini, R. and Moylan, T. (2003) 'Introduction: Dystopias and History', in R. Baccolini and T. Moylan (eds) *Dark Horizons: Science Fiction and the Dystopian Imagination* (London and New York: Routledge), 1–12

DOI: 10.1057/9781137436696.0009

Bacon, F. (2006) *New Atlantis* (Boston: Elibron Classics)

Bacon, F. (2009) *Novum Organum* (Peru, Illinois: Open Court Publishing)

Baeten, G. (2010) 'Hypochondriac Geographies of the City and the New Urban Dystopia', *City: Analysis of Urban Trends, Culture, Theory, Policy, Action*, 6(1): 103–115

Bambauer, D. (2009) 'Filtering in Oz: Australia's Foray into Internet Censorship', *University of Pennsylvania Journal of International Law*, 31(2): 493–531

Banks, I.M. (1987) *Consider Phlebas* (London: Palgrave MacMillan)

Banks, I.M. (1994) 'A Few Notes on the Culture', online at: http://trevor-hopkins.com/downloads/a-few-notes-on-the-culture.pdf. Accessed 10 February 2014

Barlow, J.P. (1996) 'A Declaration of the Independence of Cyberspace', online at: http://w2.eff.org/Censorship/Internet_censorship_bills/ barlow_0296.declaration. Accessed 16 February 2014

BBC News (2007) 'Exodus to Virtual Worlds Predicted', 11 December, online at: http://news.bbc.co.uk/1/hi/technology/7138103.stm. Accessed 23 February 2014

Baudrillard, J. (1975) *The Mirror of Production* (Candor, NY: Telos Press)

Bauman, Z. (1976) *Socialism: The Active Utopia* (London: Allen and Unwin)

Bauman, Z. (1989) *Modernity and the Holocaust* (Cambridge: Polity Press)

Bauman, Z. (2005) *Liquid Life* (Cambridge: Polity Press)

Beauchamp, G. (1986) 'Technology in the Dystopian Novel', *Modern Fiction Studies*, 32(1): 53–63

Beck, U. and Beck-Gernsheim, E. (1995) *The Normal Chaos of Love* (Cambridge: Polity Press)

Beck, U. and Beck-Gernsheim, E. (2001) *Individualization: Institutionalized Individualism and Its Social and Political Consequences* (London: Sage)

Becker, B. (2000) 'Cyborgs, Agents, and Transhumanists: Crossing Traditional Borders of Body and Identity in the Context of New Technology', *Leonardo*, 33(5): 361–365

Bell, D. (1976) *The Coming of Post-Industrial Society* (New York: Basic Books)

Bell, D., Loader, B., Pleace, N., and Schuler, D. (2004) *Cyberculture: The Key Concepts* (London: Routledge)

DOI: 10.1057/9781137436696.0009

Bellamy, E. (1996) *Looking Backward* (New York: Dover Publications)

Beniger, J. (1986) *The Control Revolution: Technological and Economic Origins of the Information Age* (Cambridge, MA: Harvard University Press)

Berman, M. (1988) *All That Is Solid Melts into Air: The Experience of Modernity*, New Edition (London: Verso)

Bessière, K., Seay, A. F., and Kiesler, S. (2007) 'The Ideal Elf: Identity Exploration in World of Warcraft', *CyberPsychology & Behavior*, 10(4): 530–535

Boas, T. (2006) 'Weaving the Authoritarian Web: The Control of Internet Use in Nondemocratic Regimes', in J. Zysman and A. Newman (eds) *How Revolutionary Was the Digital Revolution? National Responses, Market Transitions, and Global Technology* (Stanford CA: Stanford University Press), 361–378

Block, J. (2008) 'Issues for DSM-V: Internet Addiction', *American Journal of Psychiatry*, 165: 306–307

Booth, A. (1871) *Saint-Simon and Saint-Simonism: A Chapter in the History of Socialism in France* (London: Longmans, Green, Reader and Dyer)

Bort, J. (2014) 'Microsoft Explains Why Bing Offered Oddly Limited Search Results to U.S. Chinese Speakers', *Business Insider*, 11 February, online at: http://www.businessinsider.com/bing-could-be-censoring-search-results-2014-2. Accessed 8 March 2014

Brignall, T. (2002) 'The New Panopticon: The Internet Viewed as a Structure of Social Control', *Theory & Science*, 3(1): 1527–1558

Callenbach, E. (1977) *Ecotopia: The Notebooks and Reports of William Weston* (New York: Bantam Books)

Campanella, T. (2008) *The City of the Sun* (Radford, VA: Wilder Publications)

Caroti, S. (2009) 'Science Fiction, *Forbidden Planet*, and Shakespeare's *The Tempest*', in A. Yuang and C. Ross (eds) *Shakespeare in Hollywood, Asia, and Cyberspace* (West Lafayette, IN: Purdue University Press), 218–230

Castells, M. (2003) *The Internet Galaxy: Reflections on the Internet, Business, and Society* (New York: Oxford University Press)

Castells, M. (2009) *The Rise of the Network Society: Information Age: Economy, Society, and Culture v. 1*, 2nd edition (Malden, MA: Blackwell)

DOI: 10.1057/9781137436696.0009

Castells, M. (2012) *Networks of Outrage and Hope: Social Movements in the Internet Age* (Cambridge: Polity Press)

Castronova, E. (2007) *Exodus to the Virtual World: How Online Fun in Changing Reality* (New York: Palgrave Macmillan)

Centre for Internet Addiction (2014) 'FAQs', online at: http://netaddiction.com/faqs/. Accessed 10 march 2014

Chen, X. and Sin, J-C (2013) ' "Misinformation? What of it?" Motivations and Individual Differences in Misinformation Sharing on Social Media', paper presented at *ASIST 2013*, November 1–6, 2013, Montreal, Quebec, Canada

Chokoshvili, D. (2011) *The Role of the Internet in Democratic Transition: Case Study of the Arab Spring* (Budapest: Central European University)

Chomsky, N. (2006) *Failed States: The Abuse of Power and the Assault on Democracy* (New York: Metropolitan Books)

Claeys, G. and Sargent, L. (eds) (1999) *The Utopia Reader* (New York: New York University Press)

Clarke, A. (2004) *Natural-Born Cyborgs: Minds, Technologies, and the Future of Human Intelligence* (New York: Oxford University Press)

Clarke, R. (1994) 'Asimov's Laws of Robotics: Implications for Information Technology', online at: http://www.rogerclarke.com/SOS/Asimov.html#Zeroth. Accessed 11 February 2014

Cook, J. (1999) *James Cook: The Journals* (London: Penguin)

Coyne, R. (2001) *Technoromanticism: Digital Narrative, Holism and the Romance of the Real* (Boston, MA: MIT Press)

Curtis, S. (2014) 'Google Glass Haters' Attack San Francisco Woman', *The Daily Telegraph*, 26 February, online at: http://www.telegraph.co.uk/technology/news/10662112/Google-Glass-haters-attack-San-Francisco-woman.html. Accessed 11 March 2014

Cusack, C. (2009) 'Science Fiction as Scripture: Robert A. Heinlein's *Stranger in a Strange Land* and the Church of All Worlds', *Literature & Aesthetics*, 19(2): 72–91

Dahlberg, L. (2001) 'The Internet and Democratic Discourse: Exploring the Prospects of Online Deliberative Forums Extending the Public Sphere', *Information, Communication & Society*, 4(4): 615–633

Deibert, R., Palfrey, J., Rohozinski, R., and Zittrain, J. (eds) (2008) *Access Denied: The Practice and Policy of Global Internet Filtering* (Cambridge, MA: MIT Press)

Delumeau, J. (2000) *History of Paradise: The Garden of Eden in Myth and Tradition* (New York: Continuum Publishing)

Desilver, D. (2013) 'U.S. Income Inequality, on Rise for Decades, Is Now Highest since 1928', *Pew Research Center*, 5 December 2013, online at: http://www.pewresearch.org/fact-tank/2013/12/05/u-s-income-inequality-on-rise-for-decades-is-now-highest-since-1928/. Accessed 20 February 2014

DiMaggio, P. and Hargittai, E. (2001) 'From the "Digital Divide" to "Digital Inequality": Studying Internet Use as Penetration Increases', Princeton Center for Arts and Cultural Policy Studies Working Paper 15, online at: http://www.maximise-ict.co.uk/WP15_DiMaggioHargittai.pdf. Accessed 12 March 2014

Dinelo, D. (2005) *Technophobia! Science Fiction Visions of Posthuman Technology* (Austin: University of Texas Press)

Dyer-Witherford, N. (1999) *Cyber-Marx: Cycles and Circuits of Struggle in High Technology Capitalism* (Chicago: University of Illinois Press)

Eder, K. (1990) 'The Cultural Code of Modernity and the Problem of Nature: A Critique of the Naturalistic Notion of Progress', in J. Alexander and P. Sztompka (eds) *Rethinking Progress: Movements, Forces, and Ideas at the End of the Twentieth Century* (Boston, MA: Unwin Hyman), 67–87

EIU (Economist Intelligence Unit) (2012) *Democracy Index 2012*, online at: https://portoncv.gov.cv/dhub/porton.por_global.open_file?p_doc_id=1034. Accessed 16 February 2014

Ellingson, T. (2001) *The Myth of the Noble Savage* (Berkeley and Los Angeles: University of California Press)

Ellison, N., Steinfield, C., and Lampe, C. (2007) 'The Benefits of Facebook "Friends:" Social Capital and College Students' Use of Online Social Network Sites', *Journal of Computer – Mediated Communication*, 12(4): 1143–1168

Ellul, J. (1964) *The Technological Society* (Alfred A. Knopf: New York)

Ellul, J. (1980) *The Technological System* (Continuum Publishing: New York)

Ellul, J. (2005) *Perspectives on Our Age* (Toronto: Anansi)

Faris, R. and Villeneuve, N. (2008) 'Measuring Global Internet Filtering', in R. Deibert et al. (eds) *Access Denied: The Practice and Policy of Global Internet Filtering* (Cambridge, MA: MIT Press), 5–27

Feenberg, A. (1996) 'Marcuse or Habermas: Two Critiques of Technology', *Inquiry*, 39(1): 45–70

Fenton, N. (2008) 'Mediating Hope: New media, Politics and Resistance, *International Journal of Cultural Studies*, 11(2): 230–248

Ferraro, G., Caci, B., D'Amico, A., and Di Blasi, M. (2007) 'Internet Addiction Disorder: An Italian Study', *CyberPsychology & Behavior*, 10(2): 170–175

Fischer, C. (1992) *America Calling: A Social History of the Telephone* (Berkeley and Los Angeles: University of California Press)

Fishman, R. (1982) *Urban Utopias in the Twentieth Century: Ebenezer Howard, Frank Lloyd Wright, Le Corbusier* (Cambridge, MA: MIT Press)

Flacy, M. (2012) 'Study: Is Facebook More Addictive Than Alcohol or Cigarettes?' *Digital Trends*, 4 February, online at: http://www.digitaltrends.com/social-media/study-is-facebook-more-addictive-than-alcohol-or-cigarettes/#!ziQ9m. Accessed 11 March 2014

Foley, P. (2004) 'Does the Internet Help to Overcome Social Exclusion?' *Electronic Journal of E-Government*, 2(2): 139–146

Foremski, T. (2014) 'Global Edelman Survey Shows Plunging Trust in Government but Tech Industry Maintains Lead', *ZDNet*, 15 February, online at: http://www.zdnet.com/global-edelman-survey-shows-plunging-trust-in-government-but-tech-industry-maintains-lead-7000026377/. Accessed 16 February 2014

Foth, M. and Adkins, B. (2006) 'A Research Design to Build Effective Partnerships between City Planners, Developers, Government and Urban Neighbourhood Communities', *The Journal of Community Informatics*, 2(2), online at: http://ci-journal.net/index.php/ciej/article/viewArticle/292/240. Accessed 17 February 2014

Foucault, M. (1967) 'Of Other Spaces', online at: http://foucault.info/documents/heteroTopia/foucault.heteroTopia.en.html. Accessed 1 February 2014

Franklin, H. (1995) 'Introduction', in H. Franklin (ed.) *Future Perfect: American Science Fiction of the Nineteenth Century: An Anthology* (New Brunswick, NJ: Rutgers University Press)

Frazer, J. (2009) *The Golden Bough: A Study in Magic and Religion* (New York: Oxford University Press)

Friedman, T. (2013) 'Revolution Hits the Universities', *The New York Times*, 26 January, online at: http://www.nytimes.com/2013/01/27/opinion/sunday/friedman-revolution-hits-the-universities.html?_r=0. Accessed 19 February 2014

Frye, N. (1965) 'Varieties of Literary Utopias', *Daedalus*, 94(2): 323–347

DOI: 10.1057/9781137436696.0009

Fuchs, C. (2011) 'New Media, Web 2.0 and Surveillance', *Sociology Compass*, 5(2): 134–147

Fuchs, C. (2013) *Social Media: A Critical Introduction* (London: Sage)

Fukuyama, F. (1996) *Trust: The Social Virtues and the Creation of Prosperity* (New York: Simon & Schuster)

Fulcher, J. and Scott, J. (2007) *Sociology*, 3rd edition (Oxford: Oxford University Press)

Gane, N. and Sale, S. (2007) 'Interview with Friedrich Kittler and Mark Hansen', *Theory, Culture & Society*, 24(7–8): 323–329

Gardiner, M. (1992) 'Bakhtin's Carnival: Utopia as Critique', *Utopian Studies*, 3(2): 21–49

Gauntlett, D. (2011) *Making Is Connecting: The Social Meaning of Creativity, from DIY and Knitting to YouTube and Web 2.0* (Cambridge: Polity Press)

Geraci, R. (2007) 'Robots and the Sacred in Science and Science Fiction: Theological Implications of Artificial Intelligence', *Zygon*, 42(4): 961–980

Gerbaudo, P. (2012) *Tweets and the Streets: Social Media and Contemporary Activism* (London: Pluto Press)

Gershuny, J. (1993) 'Post-industrial Career Structures in Britain', in G. Esping-Andersen (ed.) *Changing Classes: Stratification and Mobility in Post-Industrial Societies* (London: Sage), 136–170

Gibson, W. ([1984] 1995) *Neuromancer* (London: Harper Voyager)

Gibson, W. (1986) *Count Zero* (New York: Victor Gollancz)

Gibson, W. (1988) *Mona Lisa Overdrive* (New York: Victor Gollancz)

Giddens, A. (1991) *Modernity and Self-identity: Self and Society in the Late Modern Age* (Cambridge: Polity Press)

Glover, J. (2001) *Humanity: A Moral History of the Twentieth Century* (London: Pimlico)

Goldman, A. (2013) 'Ray Kurzweil Says We're Going to Live Forever', *The New York Times*, 25 January, online at: http://www.nytimes.com/2013/01/27/magazine/ray-kurzweil-says-were-going-to-live-forever.html?_r=0. Accessed 24 February 2014

Goldman, L. (2005) 'This Is Your Brain on Clicks', *Forbes*, 5 August, online at: http://members.forbes.com/forbes/2005/0509/054.html. Accessed 10 March 2014

Goldring, C. (2013) 'Man or Cyborg: Does Google Glass Mark the End of True Humanity?' *The Huffington Post*, 22 July, online at:

DOI: 10.1057/9781137436696.0009

http://www.huffingtonpost.com/cassie-goldring/man-or-cyborg-does-google_b_3635068.html. Accessed 24 February 2014

Goldstone, J. (2002) 'Efflorescences and Economic Growth in World History: Rethinking the" Rise of the West" and the Industrial Revolution', *Journal of World History*, 13(2): 323–389

Google (2014) 'Transparency Report', online at: http://www.google.com/transparencyreport/removals/government/countries/. Accessed 8 March 2014

Gotham, K. (2005) 'Tourism from Above and Below: Globalization, Localization and New Orleans's Mardi Gras', *International Journal of Urban and Regional Research*, 29(2): 309–26

Greenwald, G. (2013) 'NSA Collecting Phone Records of Millions of Verizon Customers Daily', *The Guardian*, 6 June, online at: http://www.theguardian.com/world/2013/jun/06/nsa-phone-records-verizon-court-order. Accessed 8 March 2014

Greenwald, G. and MacAskill, E. (2013) 'NSA Prism Program Taps in to User Data of Apple, Google and Others', *The Guardian*, 7 June, online at: http://www.theguardian.com/world/2013/jun/06/us-tech-giants-nsa-data. Accessed 8 March 2014

Grossman, L. (2000) *The Electronic Republic: Reshaping American Democracy for the Information Age* (New York: Penguin)

Hardt, M. and Negri, A. (2001) *Empire* (Cambridge, MA: Harvard University Press)

Hargittai, E. (2011) 'Minding the Digital Gap: Why Understanding Digital Inequality Matters', in S. Papathanassopoulos (ed.) *Media Perspectives for the 21 Century* (Abingdon: Routledge), 231–240

Harris, J. (2001) 'General Introduction' in F. Tönnies (ed.) *Community and Civil Society* (Cambridge: Cambridge University Press)

Harris, M. (2011) *Sacred Folly: A New History of the Feast of Fools* (Ithaca and London: Cornell University Press)

Hassan, K. (2012) 'Making Sense of the Arab Spring: Listening to the Voices of Middle Eastern Activists', *Development*, 55(2): 232–238

Heidegger, M. (1977) *Being and Time* (Malden, MA: Blackwell-Wiley)

Heidegger, M. (1978) 'The Question Concerning Technology', *Basic Writings* (London: Routledge), 307–342

Heilbroner, R. (1967) 'Do Machines Make History?' *Technology and Culture*, 8(3): 335–345

DOI: 10.1057/9781137436696.0009

Heilbroner, R. (1994) 'Technological Determinism Revisited', in
    M. Smith and L. Marx (eds) *Does Technology Drive History? The Dilemma
    of Technological Determinism* (Cambridge, MA: MIT Press), 67–78

Heim, M. (1993) *The Metaphysics of Virtual Reality* (Oxford and New
    York: Oxford University Press)

Heinlein, R. (1961) *Stranger in a Strange Land* (New York: Putnam)

HM Government (2014) 'All E-Petitions', online at: http://epetitions.
    direct.gov.uk/petitions. Accessed 16 February 2014

Hollis, M. (1985) 'Of Masks and Men', in M. Carrithers, S. Collins, and
    S. Lukes (eds) *The Category of the Person. Anthropology, Philosophy,
    History* (Cambridge: Cambridge University Press), 217–233

Honneth, A. (2004) 'Organized Self-Realization: Some Paradoxes of
    Individualization', *European Journal of Social Theory*, 7(4): 463–478

Hout, M., Brooks, C., and Manza, J. (1993) 'The Persistence of Classes in
    Post-Industrial Societies', *International Sociology*, 8(3): 259–277

Huxley, A. (1932) *Brave New World* (London: Chatto and Windus)

IPSOS (2013) 'Socialogue: The Most Common Butterfly on Earth Is the
    Social Butterfly', 8 January, online at: http://ipsos-na.com/news-polls/
    pressrelease.aspx?id=5954. Accessed 11 March 2014

Itskov, D. (2012) 'The Path to Neo-Humanity as the Foundation of the
    Ideology of the "Evolution 2045" Party', 16 November, online at:
    http://2045.com/articles/30869.html. Accessed 24 February 2014

IWS (Internet World Stats) (2014) 'Internet Usage Statistics', online
    at: http://www.internetworldstats.com/stats.htm. Accessed 12 March
    2014

Jacobs, A. (2009) 'The Ambiguous Utopia of Iain M. Banks', *The New
    Atlantis*, online at: http://www.thenewatlantis.com/docLib/20091001_
    TNA25Jacobs.pdf. Accessed 10 February 2014

Jacobs, J. (1961) *The Death and Life of Great American Cities* (New York:
    Random House)

Jacobsen, M. and Tester, K. (2012) 'Introduction: Utopia as a Topic
    for Social Theory', in M. Jacobsen and K. Tester (eds) *Utopia: Social
    Theory and the Future* (Farnham: Ashgate)

Jarrett, K. (2008) 'Interactivity Is Evil! A Critical Investigation of Web
    2.0', *First Monday*, 13(3), online at: http://firstmonday.org/ojs/index.php/
    fm/article/view/2140/1947. Accessed 7 March 2014

Jay, M. (1996) *The Dialectical Imagination: A History of the Frankfurt School and the Institute of Social Research, 1923–1950* (Berkeley/Los Angeles: University of California Press)

Jurgenson, N. (2012) 'When Atoms Meet Bits: Social Media, the Mobile Web and Augmented Revolution', *Future Internet*, 4: 83–91

Kalathil, S. and Boas, T. (2001) 'The Internet and State Control in Authoritarian Regimes: China, Cuba, and the Counterrevolution', *First Monday*, 6(8), online at: http://www.firstmonday.dk/ojs/index.php/fm/article/view/876/785. Accessed 8 March 2014

Kang, C. (2013) 'Google to Use Balloons to Provide Free Internet Access to Remote or Poor Areas', *The Washington Post*, 15 June, online at: http://www.washingtonpost.com/business/technology/google-to-use-balloons-to-provide-internet-access-to-remote-areas/2013/06/14/f9d78196-d507-11e2-a73e-826d299ff459_story.html. Accessed 21 February 2014

Kanter, R. (1972) *Commitment and Community: Communes and Utopias in Sociological Perspective* (Cambridge, MA: Harvard University Press)

Kapor, M. (1993) 'Where Is the Digital Highway Really Heading? The Case for a Jeffersonian Information Policy', *Wired*, 1(3), online at: http://www.wired.com/wired/archive/1.03/kapor.on.nii_pr.html. Accessed 17 February 2014

Karlova, N. and Fisher, K. (2013) 'A Social Diffusion Model of Misinformation and Disinformation for Understanding Human Information Behaviour', *Information Research*, 18(1), online at: http://informationr.net/ir/18-1/paper573.html. Accessed 7 March 2014

Kateb, G. (1963) *Utopia and It's Enemies* (The Free Press: New York)

Keen, A. (2008) *The Cult of the Amateur: How Blogs, MySpace, YouTube and the Rest of Today's User-Generated Media are Killing our Culture and Economy* (Boston/London: Nicholas Brearley Publishing)

Keldoulis, I. (2004) 'Where Good Wi-Fi Makes Good Neighbors', *The New York Times*, 21 October, online at: http://www.nytimes.com/2004/10/21/technology/circuits/21spot.html?_r=0. Accessed 18 February 2014

Kennedy, J. (1992) *The New Anthropomorphism* (Cambridge: Cambridge University Press)

Khan, U. (2009) 'Twitter Should Win Nobel Peace Prize, Says Former US Security Adviser', *The Daily Telegraph*, 7 July 2009

DOI: 10.1057/9781137436696.0009

Khomani, N. (2014) '2029: The Year when Robots Will Have the Power to Outsmart Their Makers', *The Guardian*, 22 February, online at: http://www.theguardian.com/technology/2014/feb/22/ computers-cleverer-than-humans-15-years. Accessed 23 February 2014

Koch, A. (1993) 'Rationality, Romanticism and the Individual: Max Weber's "Modernism" and the Confrontation with "Modernity"', *Canadian Journal of Political Science*, 26(1): 123–144

Kolowich, S. (2012) 'Who Takes MOOCs?' *Inside Higher Ed*, 5 June, online at: http://www.insidehighered.com/news/2012/06/05/early-demographic-data-hints-what-type-student-takes-mooc. Accessed 12 March 2014

Kowalski, R., Limber, S., Limber, S. P., and Agatston, P. (2012) *Cyberbullying: Bullying in the Digital Age*, 2nd edition (Malden, MA: Blackwell-Wiley)

Kraut, R., Patterson, M., Lundmark, V., Kiesler, S., Mukophadhyay, T., and Scherlis, W. (1998) 'Internet Paradox: A Social Technology That Reduces Social Involvement and Psychological Well-Being?' *American Psychologist*, 53(9): 1017–1031

Krier, J. and Gillette, C. (1985) 'The Un-Easy Case for Technological Optimism', *Michigan Law Review*, 84(3): 405–429

Kristofferson, K., White, K., and Peloza, J. (2014) 'The Nature of Slacktivism: How the Social Observability of an Initial Act of Token Support Affects Subsequent Prosocial Action', *Journal of Consumer Research*, 40(6): 1149–1166

Kumar, K. (1991) *Utopianism* (Buckingham: Open University Press)

Kumar, K. (1997) *Utopia and Anti-utopia in Modern Times* (Oxford: Wiley: Blackwell)

Kurzweil, R. and Grossman, T. (2005) *Fantastic Voyage: Live Long Enough to Live Forever* (Emmaus: Rodale Books)

Landon, B. (2002) *Science Fiction after 1900: From the Steam Man to the Stars* (London: Routledge)

Lane, A. (2013) 'The Potential of MOOCs to Widen Access to, and Success in, Higher Education Study', paper presented at The Open and Flexible Higher Education Conference 2013, 23–25 October 2013, Paris, EADTU

Lasch, C. (1979) *The Culture of Narcissism: American Life in an Age of Diminishing Expectations* (New York: Norton)

DOI: 10.1057/9781137436696.0009

Lawner, K. (2002) 'Post-Sept. 11th International Surveillance Activity – A Failure of Intelligence: The Echelon Interception System & the Fundamental Right to Privacy in Europe', *Pace International Law Review*, 14(2): 435–480

Leary, T. (1994) *Chaos and Cyber Culture* (Berkeley, CA: Ronin Publications)

Lee, Y. and Hsieh, G. (2013) 'Does Slacktivism Hurt Activism? The Effects of Moral Balancing and Consistency in Online Activism', in *Proceedings of the SIGCHI Conference on Human Factors in Computing Systems* (ACM), 811–820

Le Guin, U. (1969) *The Left Hand of Darkness* (New York: Ace Books)

Lewin, T. (2012) 'Instruction for Masses Knocks Down Campus Walls', *The New York Times*, 4 March, online at: http://www.nytimes.com/2012/03/05/education/moocs-large-courses-open-to-all-topple-campus-walls.html?pagewanted=all. Accessed 21 February 2014

Levitas, R. (2011) *The Concept of Utopia* (New York: Peter Lang)

Liebersohn, H. (1994) 'Discovering Indigenous Nobility: Tocqueville, Chamisso, and Romantic Travel Writing', *The American Historical Review*, 99(3): 746–766

Lippens, R. (2002) 'Imachinations of Peace: Scientifictions of Peace in Iain M. Banks's *The Player of Games*', *Utopian Studies*, 13(1) (2002): 135–147

Loader, B. (ed.) (1998) *Cyberspace Divide: Equality, Agency and Policy in the Information Society* (London: Routledge)

Lodge, D. (2012) *A Man of Parts* (London: Vintage)

Loomis, C. and McKinney, J. (2003) 'Introduction: Tönnies and His Relation to Sociology' in F. Tönnies (ed.) *Community and Society* (Mineola: Dover Publications), 1–30

Löwy, M. and Sayre, R. (2001) *Romanticism Against the Tide of Modernity* (Durham NC/London: Duke University Press)

Lunau, K. (2013) 'Google's Ray Kurzweil on the Quest to Live Forever', *Maclean's*, 14 October, online at: http://www2.macleans.ca/2013/10/14/how-nanobots-will-help-the-immune-system-and-why-well-be-much-smarter-thanks-to-machines-2/. Accessed 24 February 2014

Lyon, P. (1961) 'Saint-Simon and the Origins of Scientism and Historicism', *The Canadian Journal of Economics and Political Science*, 27(1): 55–63

Lyotard, J-F (1984) *The Postmodern Condition: A Report on Knowledge* (Manchester: Manchester University Press)

DOI: 10.1057/9781137436696.0009

Mackinnon, M. (2001) 'Max Weber's Disenchantment: Lineages of Kant and Channing', *Journal of Classical Sociology*, 1(3): 329–351

Maley, T. (2013) 'Max Weber and the Iron Cage of Technology', *Bulletin of Science, Technology & Society*, 24(1): 69–86

Malmgrem, C. (1991) *Worlds Apart: Narratology in Science Fiction* (Bloomington, IN: Indian University Press)

Mannheim, K. (1997) *Ideology and Utopia: An Introduction to the Sociology of Knowledge* (New York: Routledge)

Marcuse, H. ([1964]2007) *One Dimensional Man: Studies in the Ideology of Advanced Industrial Society* (London: Routledge)

Marks, P. (2005) 'Imagining Surveillance: Utopian Visions and Surveillance Studies', *Surveillance & Society*, 3(2/3): 222–239

Marx, K. and Engels, F. (2004) *The German Ideology* (London: Lawrence & Wishart)

Matheson, R. (1954) *I Am Legend* (Robbinsdale: Fawcett Publications)

Mathiesen, T. (2013) *Towards a Surveillant Society: The Rise of Surveillance Systems ion Europe* (Hook: Waterside Press)

McGann, J. (1985) *The Romantic Ideology: A Critical Investigation* (London: The University of Chicago Press)

McGuire, M. (2010) 'Online Surveillance and Personal Liberty', in Y. Jewkes and M. Yar (eds) *Handbook of Internet Crime* (Cullompton: Willan), 492–519

McMillan, G. (2013) 'Anti-Google Glass Campaign "Stop the Cyborgs" Launches', *Digital Trends*, 25 March, online at: http://www.digitaltrends.com/computing/anti-google-glass-stop-the-cyborgs-campaign-launches/#!ziTy0. Accessed 11 March 2014

Meale, D. (2013) 'A Triple Strike against Piracy as the Music Industry Secures Three More Blocking Injunctions', *Journal of Intellectual Property Law & Practice*, 8(8): 591–594

Miller, V. (2011) *Understanding Digital Culture* (London: Sage)

Miller, V. (2012) 'A Crisis of Presence: On-line Culture and Being in the World', *Space and Polity*, 16(3): 265–285

Miller, W.M. (1960) *A Canticle for Leibowitz* (London: Weidenfield and Nicholson)

Mitchell, A. (2013) 'The Underlying Inequality of MOOCs', *eLearning Africa*, 27 August, online at: http://www.elearning-africa.com/eLA_Newsportal/the-underlying-inequality-of-moocs/. Accessed 12 March 2014

DOI: 10.1057/9781137436696.0009

Moravec, H. (2000) *Robots: Mere Machine to Transcendent Mind* (Oxford: Oxford University Press)

Morozov, E. (2012) *The Net Delusion: How Not to Liberate the World* (London: Penguin)

Morris, D. (2001) 'Direct Democracy and the Internet', *Loyola of Los Angeles Law Review*, 34(3): 1033–1054

Mossberger, K., Tolbert, C., and Stansbury, M. (2003) *Virtual Inequality: Beyond the Digital Divide* (Washington DC: Georgetown University Press)

Mumford, L. (1922) *The Story of Utopias* (New York: Boni and Liveright)

Nabatchi, T. (2010) 'Addressing the Citizenship and Democratic Deficits: The Potential of Deliberative Democracy for Public Administration', *The American Review of Public Administration*, 40(4): 376–399

Nakamura, L. (2001) 'Race in/for Cyberspace: Identity Tourism and Racial Passing on the Internet', in D. Trend (ed.) *Reading Digital Culture* (Malden, MA: Blackwell), 226–235

Norris, P. (2005) 'The Impact of the Internet on Political Activism: Evidence from Europe', *International Journal of Electronic Government Research*, 1(1): 19–39

NUA Internet Statistics (2003) 'How Many Online', online at www.nua. ie/surveys/how_many_online/. Accessed 2 January 2013

OECD (2011) *An Overview of Growing Income Inequalities in OECD Countries: Main Findings*, online at: www.oecd.org/els/social/inequality. Accessed 12 march 2014

OECD (2012) 'Life Expectancy and Healthy Life Expectancy at Age 65', in *Health at a Glance: Europe 2012* (Paris: OECD Publishing), 18–20

OECD (2014) 'OECD Broadband Statistics Update', 9 January, online at: http://www.oecd.org/sti/broadband/broadband-statistics-update.htm. Accessed 12 March 2014

Ollman, B. (2004) 'Marx's Vision of Communism', online at: http://www. nyu.edu/projects/ollman/docs/vision_of_communism.php. Accessed 7 February 2014

OLPC (One Laptop Per Child) (2014) 'Mission', online at: http://one. laptop.org/about/mission. Accessed 21 February 2014

Orlowski, A. (2013) 'Brit ISPs Ordered to Add More Movie-Streaming Websites to Block List', *The Register*, 14 November, online at: http:// www.theregister.co.uk/2013/11/14/studios_win_movie_streaming_ blocks_in_uk/. Accessed 8 March 2014

DOI: 10.1057/9781137436696.0009

P2P Foundation (2009) 'Neighbornode', online at: http://p2pfoundation.
net/Neighbornode. Accessed 18 February 2014

Park, N., Kee, K., and Valenzuela, S. (2009) 'Being Immersed in
Social Networking Environment: Facebook Groups, Uses and
Gratifications, and Social Outcomes', *CyberPsychology & Behavior*,
12(6): 729–733

Parrinder, P. (1980) *Science Fiction: Its Criticism and Teaching* (London
and New York: Methuen)

Parrinder, P. (1997) 'Eugenics and Utopia: Sexual Selection from Galton
to Morris', *Utopian Studies*, 8(2): 1–12

Paul, D. (1984) 'Eugenics and the Left', *Journal of the History of Ideas*,
45(4): 567–590

Perelman, M. (1988) *Class Warfare in the Information Age* (New York: St.
Martin's Press)

Phillips, N. and Strobl, S. (2013) *Comic Book Crime: Truth, Justice and the
American Way* (New York: New York University Press)

Phillips, W. (2011) 'LOLing at Tragedy: Facebook Trolls, Memorial Pages
and Resistance to Grief Online', *First Monday*, 16(12), online at: http://
firstmonday.org/ojs/index.php/fm/article/view/3168/3115. Accessed 10
March 2014

Pippin, R. (1995) 'On the Notion of Technology as Ideology', in A.
Feenberg and A. Hannay (eds) *Technology and the Politics of Knowledge*
(Bloomington, IN: Indiana University Press), 43–61

Platt, C. (1995) 'Superhumanism', *Wired*, 3(10), online at: http://www.
wired.com/wired/archive/3.10/moravec_pr.html. Accessed 18 March
2014

Popper, K. (2011) *The Open Society and Its Enemies* (Abingdon:
Routledge)

Posner, R. (2000) 'Orwell versus Huxley: Economics, Technology,
Privacy, and Satire', *Philosophy and Literature*, 24(1): 1–33

Price, H. and Tallinn, J. (2012) 'Artificial Intelligence – Can We Keep
It in the Box?' online at: http://theconversation.com/artificial-
intelligence-can-we-keep-it-in-the-box-8541. Accessed 21 March
2014

Putnam, R. (2000) *Bowling Alone: The Collapse and Revival of American
Community* (New York: Simon & Schuster)

Puzzanghera, J. (2014) 'Oxfam Report Highlights Widening Income Gap
between Rich, Poor', *Los Angeles Times*, 20 January, online at: http://

DOI: 10.1057/9781137436696.0009

www.latimes.com/business/la-fi-income-inequality-20140121,0,3481555.
story. Accessed 20 February 2014

Quayle, E., Vaughan, M., and Taylor, M. (2006) 'Sex Offenders, Internet
Child Abuse Images and Emotional Avoidance: The Importance of
Values', *Aggression and Violent Behavior*, 11(1): 1–11

Raine, L. and Wellman, B. (2012) *Networked: The New Social Operating
System* (Cambridge, MA: MIT Press)

Reporters without Borders (2013) 'Special Report on Internet
Surveillance', 15 March, online at: http://en.rsf.org/special-report-on-
internet-11-03-2013,44197.html. Accessed 8 March 2014

Rheingold, H. (1993) *The Virtual Community: Finding Connection in a
Computerized World* (New York: Addison-Wesley Longman)

Riley, J. (2001) *Rising Life Expectancy: A Global History* (Cambridge:
Cambridge University Press)

Roberts, A. (2000) *Science Fiction* (London: Routledge)

Roberts, R. (1971) *The New Communes: Coming Together in America* (New
Jersey: Prentice Hall)

Robinson, A. and Karatzogianni, A. (2012) 'Digital Prometheus:
WikiLeaks, the State-Network Dichotomy and the Antinomies
of Academic Reason', online at: http://works.bepress.com/athina_
karatzogianni/15. Accessed 16 February 2014

Rohrbach, D. (2009) 'Sector Bias and Sector Dualism: The Knowledge
Society and Inequality', *International Journal of Comparative Sociology*,
50(5–6): 510–536

Rumpala, Y. (2011) 'Artificial Intelligences and Political Organization:
An Exploration Based on the Science Fiction Work of Iain
M. Banks', online at: http://www.inter-disciplinary.net/wp-content/
uploads/2011/06/rumpalaepaper.pdf. Accessed 11 February 2014

Sargent, L. (2010) *Utopianism: A Very Short Introduction* (New York:
Oxford University Press)

Schaller, B. (1996) 'The Origin, Nature, and Implications of "MOORE'S
LAW"', online at: http://research.microsoft.com/en-us/um/people/gray/
Moore_Law.html. Accessed 9 February 2014

Seed, D. (2003) 'Cyberpunk and Dystopia: Pat Cadigan's Networks', in
R. Baccolini and T. Moylan (eds) *Dark Horizons: Science Fiction and
the Dystopian Imagination* (New York: Routledge)

Sennett, R. (1977) *The Fall of Public Man* (New York: Alfred A. Knopf)

Shah, D. (2013) 'MOOCs in 2013: Breaking Down the Numbers: Teasing
Out Trends Among the Unabated Growth of Online Courses', 22

DOI: 10.1057/9781137436696.0009

December, online at: https://www.edsurge.com/n/2013–12-22-moocs-
in-2013-breaking-down-the-numbers. Accessed 21 February 2014

Shute, N. (1957) *On the Beach* (London: Heineman)

Sibley, M. (1973) 'Utopian Thought and Technology', *American Journal of
Political Science*, 17(2): 255–281

Simon, W. (1956) 'History for Utopia: Saint-Simon and the Idea of
Progress', *Journal of the History of Ideas*, 17(3): 311–331

Sippel, A. (2006) 'The Machine in the Pastoral Imagery of Eighteenth-
Century Utopias', *Spaces of Utopia: An Electronic Journal*, 3: 27–37

Skinner, B.F. (1948) *Walden Two* (Indianapolis: Hackett)

Slater, T. (2002) 'Fear of the City 1882–1967: Edward Hopper and the
Discourse of Anti-Urbanism', *Social & Cultural Geography*, 3(2):
135–154

Sloterdijk, P. (2009) '*Rules for the Human Zoo:* A Response to the *Letter
on Humanism*', *Environment & Planning D: Society and Space*, 27: 12–28

Smith, P.D. (2012) *City: A Guidebook for the Urban Age* (London:
Bloomsbury Publishing)

Spar, D. (1999) 'The Public Face of Cyberspace', in I. Kaul, I. Grunberg,
and M. Stern (eds) *Global Public Goods: International Cooperation in
the 21st Century* (New York: Oxford University Press), 344–362

Stedman-Jones, G. (2006) 'Saint-Simon and the Liberal Origins of the
Socialist Critique of Political Economy' in S. Aprile and F. Bensimon
(eds) *La France et l'Angleterre au XIXe siècle: Échanges, représentations,
comparaisons*: 21–47 (Paris: Créaphis)

Stein, J. (2004) 'The Telephone: Its Social Shaping and Public
Negotiation in Late Nineteenth- and Early Twentieth Century
London', in M. Crang, P. Crang and J. May (eds) *Virtual Geographies:
Bodies, Space and Relations* (London: Routledge), 44–62

Stepanova, E. (2011) 'The Role of Information Communication
Technologies in the "Arab Spring"', PONARS Eurasia Policy Memo
No. 159, May, online at: http://www.gwu.edu/~ieresgwu/assets/docs/
ponars/pepm_159.pdf. Accessed 17 February 2014

Stephenson, N. (1995) *The Diamond Age: Or, a Young Lady's Illustrated
Primer* (New York: Bantam)

Stevens, J. (1988) *Storming Heaven: LSD and the American Dream*
(London: Harper)

Stevenson, C. (2007) 'Breaching the Great Firewall: China's Internet
Censorship and the Quest for Freedom of Expression in a Connected

World', *Boston College International and Comparative Law Review*, 30(2): 531–558

Stiglitz, J. (1999) 'Knowledge as a Global Public Good', in I. Kaul, I. Grunberg, and M. Stern (eds) *Global Public Goods: International Cooperation in the 21 Century* (New York: Oxford University Press), 308–325

Stoll, C. (2000) *Hi-Tech Heretic: Reflections of a Computer Contrarian* (New York: Anchor Books)

Suler, J. (2004) 'The Online Disinhibition Effect', *Cyberpsychology & Behavior*, 7(3): 321–326

Sutter, J. (2012) 'Google Reports 'Alarming' Rise in Government Censorship Requests', CNN, 19 June, online at: http://edition.cnn.com/2012/06/18/tech/web/google-transparency-report/. Accessed 8 March 2014

Tampio, N. (2009) 'Assemblages and the Multitude: Deleuze, Hardt, Negri, and the Postmodern Left', *European Journal of Political Theory*, 8(3): 383–400

Tancons, E. (2011) 'Occupy Wall Street: Carnival Against Capital? Carnivalesque as Protest Sensibility', e-flux, 30, online at: http://www.e-flux.com/journal/occupy-wall-street-carnival-against-capital-carnivalesque-as-protest-sensibility/. Accessed 2 February 2014

Taylor, C. (2002) 'Modern Social Imaginaries', *Public Culture* 14(1): 91–124

Telotte, J. (1991) 'The Tremulous Public Body: Robots, Change and the Science Fiction Film', *Journal of Popular Film and Television*, 19(1): 14–23

Thompson, J. (1984) *Studies in the Theory of Ideology* (Cambridge: Polity Press)

The Economist (2013) 'The Attack of the MOOCs', 20 July, online at: http://www.economist.com/news/business/21582001-army-new-online-courses-scaring-wits-out-traditional-universities-can-they. Accessed 12 March 2014

Thompson, J. (2005) 'The New Visibility', *Theory, Culture & Society*, 22(6): 31–51

Tilman, R. (1985) 'The Utopian Vision of Edward Bellamy and Thorstein Veblen', *Journal of Economic Issues*, 19(4): 879–898

Tocqueville, A. ([1835(2003)]) *Democracy in America: And Two Essays on America* (London: Penguin)

DOI: 10.1057/9781137436696.0009

Toffler, A. (1980) *The Third Wave* (New York: Bantam Books)

Tönnies, F. ([1887]2003) *Community and Society* (Mineola: Dover Publications)

Tönnies, F. ([1935]2010) *Geist der Neuzeit* (Munich/Vienna: Profil Verlag)

Trahair, R. (1999) *Utopias and Utopians: An Historical Dictionary* (Westport, CT: Greenwood Press)

Trentmann, F. (1994) 'Civilization and Its Discontents: English Neo-Romanticism and the Transformation of Anti-Modernism in Twentieth-Century Western Culture', *Journal of Contemporary History*, 29(4): 583–625

Turkle, S. (1997) *Life On the Screen: Identity in The Age of the Internet* (London: Weidenfeld & Nicholson)

Turkle, S. (2011) *Alone Together: Why We Expect More from Technology and Less from Each Other* (New York: Basic Books)

Twenge, J. and Campbell, W. (2009) *The Narcissism Epidemic: Living in an Age of Entitlement* (New York: Atira)

Valkenburg, P., Peter, J., and Schouten, A. (2006) 'Friend Networking Sites and Their Relationship to Adolescents' Well-Being and Social Self-Esteem', *CyberPsychology & Behavior*, 9(5): 584–590

Verton, D. (2003) *Black Ice: The Invisible Threat of Cyber-Terrorism* (Emeryville, CA: McGraw-Hill/Osborne)

Vinge, V. (1993) 'The Coming Technological Singularity: How to Survive in the Post-Human Era', online at: http://www-rohan.sdsu.edu/faculty/vinge/misc/singularity.html. Accessed 11 February 2014

Virilio, P. (2012) *The Administration of Fear* (Los Angeles, CA: Semiotext(e))

Vonnegut, K. (1952) *Player Piano* (New York: Charles Scribner's Sons)

Waldrop, M. (2013) 'Massive Open Online Courses, aka MOOCs, Transform Higher Education and Science', *Scientific American*, 13 March, online at: http://www.scientificamerican.com/article/massive-open-online-courses-transform-higher-education-and-science/. Accessed 19 February 2014

Wall, T. and Monahan, T. (2011) 'Surveillance and Violence from Afar: The Politics of Drones and Liminal Security-Scapes', *Theoretical Criminology*, 15(3): 239–254

Waltz, D. (1988) 'The Prospects for Building Truly Intelligent Machines', *Daedalus*, 117(1): 191–212

DOI: 10.1057/9781137436696.0009

Ward, S., Gibson, R., and Lusoli, W. (2003) 'Online Participation and Mobilisation in Britain: Hype, Hope and Reality', *Parliamentary Affairs*, 56: 652–668

Webb, D. (2005) 'Bakhtin at the Seaside: Utopia, Modernity and the Carnivalesque', *Theory, Culture & Society*, 22(3): 121–138

Weber, M. (1991) 'Science as Vocation', in H. Gerth and C.W. Mills (eds) *From Max Weber: Essays in Sociology* (London: Routledge), 129–156

Weber, M. (2005) 'Remarks on Technology and Culture', *Theory, Culture & Society*, 22(4): 23–38

Webster, F. (2006) *Theories of the Information Society*. 3rd edition (London: Routledge)

Weise, E. (2014) 'San Francisco Bar Bans "Glassholes" ', *USA Today*, 5 March, online at: http://www.usatoday.com/story/tech/2014/03/05/san-francisco-bar-bans-google-glass-glassholes/6080801/. Accessed 11 March 2014

Wells, H.G. (1901) *Anticipations of the Reaction of Mechanical and Scientific Progress upon Human Life and Thought* (London: Harper)

Wells, H.G. (1905) *A Modern Utopia* (London: Chapman & Hall)

Wells, H.G. (1923) *Men Like Gods* (New York: Ferris)

Westfahl, G, Palumbo, D., and Sullivan, C. (eds) (2007) *Hugo Gernsback and the Century of Science Fiction* (Jefferson, NC: McFarland & Co)

Whitty, M. and Buchanan, T. (2012) 'The Online Romance Scam: A Serious Cybercrime', *CyberPsychology, Behavior, and Social Networking*, 15(3): 181–183

Wiggershaus, R. (1995) *The Frankfurt School: Its History, Theories and Significance* (Cambridge: Polity Press)

Wikileaks (2014) 'About', online at: http://wikileaks.org/About.html. Accessed 16 February 2014

Williams, R. (1973) *The Country and the City* (Oxford: Oxford University Press)

Williams, R. (1978) 'Utopia and Science Fiction', *Science Fiction Studies*, 5(3): 203–214

Wilson, N. (1992) 'The Name Hythlodaeus', *Moreana*, 29, 110: 33

Winner, L. (1977) *Autonomous Technology: Technics-out-of-Control as a Theme in Political Thought* (Boston, MA: MIT Press)

Yar, M. (2008) 'The Rhetorics and Myths of Anti-Piracy Campaigns: Criminalization, Moral Pedagogy and Capitalist Property Relations in the Classroom', *New Media & Society*, 10(4): 605–623

DOI: 10.1057/9781137436696.0009

Yar, M. (2012a) 'Crime, Media and the Will-to-Representation: Reconsidering Relationships in the New Media Age', *Crime Media Culture*, 8(3): 245–260

Yar, M. (2012b) 'E-Crime 2.0: The Criminological Landscape of New Social Media', *Information & Communication Technology Law*, 21(3): 207–219

Yar, M. (2013) *Cybercrime and Society.* 2nd edition (London: Sage)

Young, K. and Rodgers, R. (1998) 'The Relationship between Depression and Internet Addiction', *CyberPsychology & Behavior*, 1(1): 25–28

Zhuo, J. (2010) 'Where Anonymity Breeds Contempt', *The New York Times*, 29 November, online at: http://www.nytimes.com/2010/11/30/opinion/30zhuo.html?_r=0. Accessed 10 March 2014

Ziolkowski, T. (2000) *The Sin of Knowledge: Ancient Themes and Modern Variations* (Princeton, NJ: Princeton University Press)

Zuckerberg, M. (2014) 'Is Connectivity a Human Right?' online at: https://fbcdn-dragon-a.akamaihd.net/hphotos-ak-ash3/851575_22879423 3937224_51579300_n.pdf. Accessed 21 February 2014

DOI: 10.1057/9781137436696.0009

Index

DOI: 10.1057/9781137436696.0010

DOI: 10.1057/9781137436696.0010

DOI: 10.1057/9781137436696.0010

DOI: 10.1057/9781137436696.0010

DOI: 10.1057/9781137436696.0010

Printed in the USA
CPSIA information can be obtained
at www.ICGtesting.com
LVHW101207300723
753506LV00023B/27